The Princeton Review

Math Smart

Junior

Math You'll Understand

Books in The Princeton Review Series

Cracking the ACT
Cracking the ACT with Sample Tests on Computer Disk
Cracking the GED
Cracking the GMAT
Cracking the GMAT with Sample Tests on Computer Disk
Cracking the GRE
Cracking the GRE with Sample Tests on Computer Disk
Cracking the GRE Psychology Subject Test
Cracking the LSAT
Cracking the LSAT with Sample Tests on Computer Disk
Cracking the MCAT
Cracking the MCAT with Sample Tests on Computer Disk
Cracking the SAT and PSAT
Cracking the SAT and PSAT with Sample Tests on Computer Disk
Cracking the SAT II: Biology Subject Test
Cracking the SAT II: Chemistry Subject Test
Cracking the SAT II: English Subject Tests
Cracking the SAT II: French Subject Test
Cracking the SAT II: History Subject Tests
Cracking the SAT II: Math Subject Tests
Cracking the SAT II: Physics Subject Test
Cracking the SAT II: Spanish Subject Test
Cracking the TOEFL with Audiocassette

SAT Math Workout
SAT Verbal Workout

Don't Be a Chump!
How to Survive Without Your Parents' Money
Trashproof Resumes

Grammar Smart
Math Smart
Reading Smart
Study Smart
Word Smart: Building an Educated Vocabulary
Word Smart II: How to Build a More Educated Vocabulary
Writing Smart

Grammar Smart Junior
Math Smart Junior
Word Smart Junior
Writing Smart Junior

Student Access Guide to America's Top 100 Internships
Student Access Guide to College Admissions
Student Access Guide to the Best Business Schools
Student Access Guide to the Best Law Schools
Student Access Guide to the Best Medical Schools
Student Access Guide to the Best 309 Colleges
Student Access Guide to the Big Book of Colleges
Student Access Guide to Paying for College
Student Access Guide to Visiting College Campuses

Also available on cassette from Living Language
Grammar Smart
Word Smart
Word Smart II

The Princeton Review

Math Smart
Junior

Math You'll Understand

by Marcia Lerner and Doug McMullen, Jr.

Random House, Inc., New York 1995

Acknowledgments

For their editing and organizational expertise the authors would like to thank Hannah Fox, Bronwyn Collie, Chris Kensler, Lee Elliott, Kristin Fayne-Mulroy, P.J. Waters, and Christine Chung. They would also like to thank John Bergdahl, Adam Hurwitz, Peter Jung, Sara Kane, Meher Khambata, Illeny Maaza, Jeff Moores, Russell Murray, Glen Pannell, Dinica Quesada, Christopher D. Scott, and Ray Suhler for designing, illustrating, and producing this book.

CONTENTS

Introduction

A Very Sneaky Thing

We have done a very sneaky thing. In a very funny story about three crazy kids and a four-foot tall talking cat named Beauregard, we have hidden *math problems*.

Not Math Problems!

Yes, math problems. But don't be afraid. Each chapter tells part of the story and covers a different area of math. We start out assuming that you know how to add, subtract, multiply, and divide normal (whole) numbers. Can you solve 213 + 79? 125 ÷ 5? If you can do these kinds of math problems, you're ready to start the book. If you *do* have trouble with these kinds of problems, don't sweat it. Just turn to p. 183 and do our quick and easy grade school math review. You'll feel much better, and *then* you can plow into the new stuff.

How to Plow

Throughout each chapter are quizzes with answers and explanations so you can put what you just learned to use right away. At the end of the book is a glossary that explains math terms you might not understand. When a word is printed in extra-dark letters in the text (called **boldface**), that word is explained in the glossary.

WAIT, THERE'S MORE!

Before you start you should be prepared to do two things:

- Use scratch paper to solve the problems

- Have fun

When you're doing math problems you have to write things down because thinking about numbers can get confusing if you don't. You should have fun too because math is not the end of the world. If you take it one step at a time, you'll be amazed at how much you'll know once you reach the end of the book. You may even end up *liking* math. It could happen!

Chapter 1
Approximation

The day was scorching hot, and the kids, Sondra, Jennifer, and Taylor, were hiding from the sun beneath the wide shady branches of their favorite oak tree in the park.

"Gnuuuuuhhhhhh," Taylor groaned. He lay flat on his back and stared gloomily upward through the leaves of the oak.

"I take it that moose-call of yours means you're kinda hot," Jennifer commented.

"Gnuh-huh," Taylor nodded, "h-h-hot."

"Well, we can't just sit here and melt," Sondra said miserably. "Oh gross, I think even my *knees* are sweating."

"That's nothing, my *teeth* are sweating," Taylor said, flashing them in the sun.

"Yeah? I think the *insides of my ears* are sweating." Jennifer poked in her ear. "Yuk."

Sondra looked at her friends, "What're we gonna do?"

"Let's have a sweating contest. Whoever sweats the most from the weirdest place wins," Taylor suggested.

"Blick! You're so disgusting!" Sondra said.

Jennifer quietly poked her finger into her other ear. Then Taylor raised his arm, pointed his index finger toward the sky, and, in a very dignified way, said, "*I* am not disgusting; my *ideas* are disgusting."

"*Right.* Whatever," Jennifer said, taking her finger out of her ear. "Here's my idea, let's ride our bikes really fast through the park downhill with no hands and . . ."

Sondra and Taylor stared at Jennifer like she'd gone crazy from the heat.

"We'll go swooping back and forth like great birds of prey circling a mountaintop, it'll be like flying, like . . ."

"Crashing," Taylor interrupted, "like a flat tire, like pushing your bike uphill with bloody knees and the sun

beaming down on your skull until your brain bubbles like eggs in frying pan. Forget it. Besides, we'd probably run into that big kid Skeezer and his freaky pal Fred. I'm not moving. No way. Count me out. I vote we stay under the tree and spend the afternoon complaining. I like complaining . . . it's restful and satisfying."

"Bike riding," Jennifer insisted.

"Complaining."

"Bike riding."

"Complaining."

"Bike riding."

"Complaining."

"Bike riding."

"*Quuiiieeeettttt!*" Sondra yelled. "I'll settle this. *Compromise*, okay? Why don't we just ride our bikes, without complaining, like normal human beings having a nice time together."

Jennifer and Taylor both looked at her as if she were abnormal. They agreed it was the worst idea they'd ever heard.

"Wait a minute! I've got it," Sondra cried. "We'll have a contest. Whoever can come closest to guessing the number of leaves on the oak tree will decide what to do. *I'll be the judge.*"

"Okay," Jennifer and Taylor said. At least they were buying time. They shook on it.

Guessing amounts, such as lengths of time, or distance, or the number of leaves on a tree is called **approximation**. It is a really important tool in all kinds of math. When you approximate, you make your best guess. It doesn't have to be exactly right, just somewhere near to the answer. You probably already approximate a lot. When you jump from one rock to another in a stream, you first approximate the distance then try to jump that amount so you don't end up in the water. Approximation can help you do a lot of things. It can help you check answers, avoid doing some calculations altogether, and make you better at understanding many different things about math. Try doing some approximation with your friends at lunch, watching television, or eating dinner at home. Approximately how many hours of television do you watch a day? Approximately how many hours do you sleep a night? Approximately how many slices of blueberry pie can you eat before you feel full?

Approximately how many leaves *are* on a big oak tree? And hey, how would you ever find out how close your approximation was without actually counting? The truth is you couldn't find out *exactly* how many leaves are on an oak tree without counting, so unless you've got the time and a ladder, you can't know *exactly* how close your approximation was. With most math problems, you can't tell how close your approximations are unless you "do out" the math. But that doesn't mean some approximations aren't better than others. If you're hopping from rock to rock in a stream, you have to first use your senses to make a judgment of how far the distance is, then use your memory of past jumps to decide how much force to put in your legs. If all goes well and your judgment is good, you land on that rock. If not, well, you get wet.

With mathematical approximations the process is similar; the jump is mental (so you don't have to worry about the strength of your legs), but you do have to use your judgment and past experience to decide how far to go. The more practice you get at approximating the better you'll be at it. A good approximation will be helpful. A not-so-good one won't be helpful.

Oh, by the way, about how many glumphs are in your bwangko? If you don't know what a glumph is, or a bwangko, you won't have any idea. (At least we hope not . . . they're made-up words.) But, if we tell you that bwanko means *mouth* and glumphs are *teeth*, you can draw on your experience to make an approximation of the number. So how many teeth *are* in your mouth? Don't count. Approximate. More than 9? Less than 9?

Now, take your finger out of your ear and count your teeth. Were you close? (Kinda weird isn't it? Most people don't know how many teeth they have!) Suppose you had to approximate the number of teeth in two people's mouths, or three mouths, or one hundred mouths. Would you count? I hope not. What if you had to estimate how many grains in a cup of sand? You'd be counting a long time on that one. But by using a few simple mathematical operations (and just a little counting) you could get to a good approximation. For example, you could count the grains of sand in a teaspoonful (still quite a few), then find out how many teaspoons in a cup.

So, to help make approximations, let's quickly review whole number addition, subtraction, multiplication, and division. Those are the operations Jennifer and Taylor are going to use to help them approximate the number of leaves on the oak tree. (You didn't think they were going to count them did you?) You probably know how to do these operations already, but it's always good to practice, because for the rest of your life, no matter what career you decide to pursue, you'll have to add, subtract, multiply, and divide.

If Sondra has 3 bicycles, and Jennifer has 2 bicycles, how many bicycles do they have altogether?

Easy right? 5. But hey, since Sondra and Jennifer don't need more than 1 bicycle each, let's say we take away the extras. 5 – 3 = 2. (That's actually a more complicated problem than it sounds. We'll solve that same "easy" problem again when we look at algebra in the final chapter.)

Addition and subtraction are opposites. You can see this easily on the number line. The number line shows you how all the numbers compare. Numbers on the right are always bigger than numbers on the left. Number lines have arrows on the ends indicating that they extend to **infinity**. Infinity is shown by this symbol: . There is no end to numbers—on either end you can keep making them bigger, or smaller (that's pretty wild, right?).

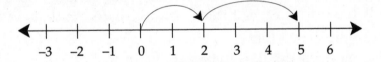

If you get confused about adding or subtracting, you can always look at a number line. Start with the number you have, then move right to add, or left to subtract. The bicycle calculations look like this on the number line:

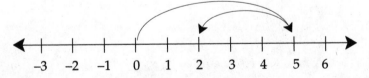

And when we take away the extra bicycles, it looks like this:

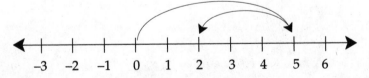

THINK ABOUT THIS

Sometimes, you have a math problem written out in word form. For instance a problem that says, "If Sondra has 1 hat, and Jennifer has 2 hats, how many hats do they have together?" actually means $1 + 2 = \underline{\hspace{1em}}$. The best way to solve these word problems is to write things down as you go. After every pause in the sentence, when you find out information about Sondra, for example, write down what you know, and label it if necessary. This way, you can easily translate a written sentence into an arithmetic problem. For example, the word "together" in the problem here tips you off that it is most likely an addition problem. Look for clues like this in all the word problems you do.

✎ ✎ ✎ ✎ ✎

Back at the oak tree Jennifer and Taylor have worked out their approximations. Here's how they did it.

Jennifer

Hmmm . . . there's about 5 leaves on every small branch.

There's about 7 small branches on each medium branch.

So 7 small branches 5 times is 35.

There's 35 leaves on every medium size branch. Okay.

Three medium size branches on every big branch. So if one medium size branch is 35, then 3 medium size branches will be 3 times 35 = 105.

105 leaves on every big branch. There's 10 big branches. So 10 times 105 is 1050.

"I figure there's 1,050 leaves on the tree!" Jennifer announced, looking pleased with herself.

Taylor

Let's see, if I divide the tree into 10 levels starting at the top, then the topmost level has 2 leaves.

The second level down has about twice that, which is 4.

The third level down is twice 4, which is 8. I think it doubles at every level so the next level down is

16 times 2 is 32
32 times 2 is 64
64 times 2 is 128
128 times 2 is 256
256 times 2 is 512
512 times 2 is 1024.

"Actually it's closer to 1,024." Taylor looked across at Jennifer.

"Is that so? Well, let's ask Sondra," said Jennifer, folding her arms and looking confident.

Sondra looked uneasily at Jennifer, "Uh ... " then at Taylor, " ... actually," then back at Jennifer, "well, it's really very simple ... "

"You don't know how many leaves are on the tree, do you?" Taylor said quietly.

He turned to Jennifer. "She doesn't know how many leaves are ... "

Jennifer glared at Sondra, "You know how many leaves are on the tree, *right?* You didn't make us waste our time figuring out how many leaves were on the oak tree when you didn't know the answer yourself, *right?*"

"No ... I mean, yes ... I mean, of course I know how many leaves are on the tree ... *of course I do* ... The problem is that both your guesses are so close I have to do some calculations of my own." Her face went red as she scribbled furiously on a piece of notebook paper for a few moments before announcing, "*Just as I thought!* It's a tie."

What Sondra really worked out was the following: "How can I make the two numbers be a tie? Let's see, if the right number of leaves is between 1,050 and 1,024, then it could tie. Okay, so what's the difference between 1,050 and 1,024?" (In a word problem the word "difference" is a clue to *subtract*.)

$$1,050 - 1,024 = 26$$

"Now if I just split the difference in half ... "

(Splitting a number in half is the same as dividing by 2.)

$$26 \div 2 \text{ is } 13$$

"Now if I add 13 to the smaller number ... "

$$13 + 1,024 = 1,037$$

"and subtract 13 from the larger number..."

$$1{,}050 - 13 = 1{,}037$$

"the answers should tie."

$$1{,}037 = 1{,}037$$

"Alright!"

✎ ✎ ✎ ✎ ✎

"There's 1,037 leaves on the tree, so you see you're both off by thirteen. Taylor estimated thirteen leaves too few, and Jennifer, you estimated thirteen too many," Sondra informed her friends.

"All that work for nothing." Taylor sighed. "What a lousy deal, I should've known it wouldn't work, nothing ever seems to work, especially in this heat."

"Well, at least nobody lost the contest. That's why ties are the best. Nobody loses," Sondra said.

"What do you mean?" Taylor demanded, his own face getting red. " If there's no winner then *everybody* loses. So in a tie, everyone loses. That makes us all *losers*. It's hopeless. Everything is hopeless. And we're still hot. And we still don't know what to do. G-nuhhhhhhhhh."

"He's doing that moose-call thing again," Jennifer said to Sondra. But Sondra didn't hear a thing; this time *she* had her pinkies in her ears. She didn't even hear the smooth, deep voice that came from a shadowy spot at the crook in a branch way up in the oak tree.

"Perhaps I can be of assistance?"

In working out their approximations of how many leaves were on the oak tree, Sondra, Taylor, and Jennifer didn't use any fancy math. All they did was add, subtract, multiply, and divide. But that doesn't mean the problems they solved were easy. Often the hardest part of a math problem is knowing what to do and when to do it. Sondra, Jennifer, and Taylor put their math problem together like real pros. Putting the steps of a math problem together so it makes sense is a valuable skill, and it's one of the things we hope you learn from this book. But first you've got to be able to do the basic operations. If you have *any* trouble understanding how to do addition, subtraction, multiplication, or division, go to the review appendix in the back of the book, for an explanation of each operation.

Chapter 2
Order of Operations

The voice in the tree came from a big ink-black cat. He lay sleepily along a thick branch with just one eye open. His long tail drooped like an upside down question mark and swayed ever so lazily in the hot afternoon air.

"Beauregard!" the kids all said at once.

"At your service," the cat replied, nodding slightly.

"Hey, how long have you been up there? Have you been up there the whole day spying on us?" Sondra demanded.

"Spying? Gracious no. Me? Heavens! I was merely cat-napping here in this tree when the three of you began to quarrel, an event which awakened me from my glorious slumber. I was dreaming, you know, fond dreams of Tabitha Mae Malone, a kitten I used to frolic with in other times ... ahhh, Tabitha ... I was having a most wonderful dream. There isn't time to go into it now, of course. Well, anyway ...

"I thought I might offer some assistance with the problem at hand. It's hot out, that's true, not that I mind. I love hot weather. But the three of you are getting, dare I say it ... cranky? So let me propose a solution."

The kids waited beneath the tree. And they kept on waiting.

Finally Jennifer yelled, "Hey! Beauregard!"

"Oh dear," the cat said, "dozed off again in this marvellous heat ... where was I? Oh yes. Lunch. That's my solution. Lunch. Why don't you all come over to my house and have lunch?" And with that, Beauregard hopped gracefully out of the tree and strolled off (on his hind legs) toward his house.

The kids turned to each other. "What're we waiting for? C'mon, let's go."

Beauregard's house wasn't far off. It was a nice normal house in most respects, with a little white fence in the front and flowers (all catnip!) in the garden. There was no garage though; Beauregard didn't drive. And of course the house was a bit small. Beauregard was only four feet tall, so the house, and everything in it, was shrunk down to his size. But of course that made it perfect for kids. Oh, and one other thing—the outside of the house was painted in tiger stripes, and all the walls inside had leopard spots. But otherwise it was a nice, normal house.

So, Beauregard turned on the air-conditioning and soon the kids were relaxing in his living room.

"Ahhh, much better," Jennifer said as she sprawled over a few cushions on the floor.

"I couldn't agree more," Sondra said, sitting up very properly in a soft chair.

"Now there's nothing left to complain about," Taylor complained happily.

"Lunch, lunch, lunch . . . hmmm . . . let me see." The kids could hear Beauregard puttering in the kitchen and talking to himself. "Mousaroni and cheese? No, not today. Mouseburger helper. Oh, but I'm tired of that."

"Maybe lunch wasn't such a good idea," Jennifer whispered.

"Mouse-meat soup? No, too much work. Fillet of mouse steak? Too fancy. Perhaps some nice simple peanut butter and mouse-guts jelly sandwiches? Ahhh . . . here we are . . ." Beauregard poked his big pointy-eared head around the doorway. "How about pizza?"

"Sure. Great. Ideal," the kids said, nodding their heads furiously.

"The only problem is we'll have to prepare it ourselves."

"No problem," the kids assured Beauregard.

"Goodness, you all seem to like pizza. Now, where did I put that recipe? Oh here it is." Beauregard showed them the recipe:

One 10-ounce tube ready-made pizza crust
3/4 cup tomato sauce
1/2 cup pepperoni slices, or sliced mushrooms, or both
1/2 cup grated mozzarella cheese
Garlic powder
1/2 cup fresh mouse heads

Preheat oven to 475° F.

Pat or roll out dough on a greased cookie sheet to make a big circle.

Spread sauce on circle, then sprinkle cheese on top of sauce. Add mushrooms and pepperoni, sprinkle with garlic powder, and bake in oven for about 20 minutes. Garnish with fresh mouse heads.

"This sounds excellent and delicious, Beauregard. But, um, about the mouse heads. You don't expect us to actually eat . . . ?" Sondra couldn't bring herself to finish the question.

"Oh, don't worry. The mouse heads are optional. Now, to me, a pizza without mouse heads is like a chocolate-chip cookie without the chips. Why bother? But, alas, I'm used to humans' strange eating habits. Peppermint candies for instance. Just imagine eating peppermint candies. Blaggghh! So you don't have to add the mouse heads if you don't want to, but just don't ever try to feed *me* peppermint candies. Okay?"

"Deal!"

The kids charged into the kitchen to help Beauregard make the pizza.

Believe it or not, math is lot like cooking. You can have all the ingredients, but if you don't put them together in the right order you can make a real mess. Imagine trying to make a pizza by first pouring out the sauce and then adding the dough! How about frosting the batter before you bake the cake! Well it happens all the time in math because people don't know the "recipe" for the problem. It is called the **order of operations**.

Here is a problem:

$$2 + (3 \times 5) - 6 \div 2 + 1(3 + 1) =$$

This problem looks so complicated it could scare anyone. But here's the secret: there is a specific order and you always use it. The order is: Parentheses, Exponents, Multiplication, Division, Addition, Subtraction. Okay, always do the stuff in the parentheses first.

$$2 + \mathbf{(3 \times 5)} - 6 \div 2 + 1\,\mathbf{(3 + 1)} =$$

becomes

$$2 + \mathbf{(15)} - 6 \div 2 + 1 \times \mathbf{(4)} =$$

The next operation is **exponents**, but there are no exponents here (phew), so multiplication and division are done next. Do them in any order you want as long as you do them <u>before</u> doing any addition or subtraction. (Most people go left to right because that's how we read.)

$$2 + (15) - 6 \div 2 + 1 \times (4) =$$

Since $6 \div 2 = 3$, and $1 \times (4) = 4$, this becomes

$$2 + (15) - 3 + 4 =$$

That leaves addition and subtraction. Do them left to right (until you understand negative numbers—which you will once you've finished this book).

$$\overrightarrow{2 + (15) - 3 + 4 =}$$

How can you remember the order of operations? Some people remember the word PEMDAS, others remember the helpful phrase using words that begin with each letter: <u>P</u>lease <u>E</u>xcuse <u>M</u>y <u>D</u>ear <u>A</u>unt <u>S</u>ally. Use whichever works.

✍ QUIZ #1 ✍
Arithmetic Check

1. $17 + 34 - 22 = $ _____. Is the answer odd or even?

2. $505 - 100 \times 3 = $ _____. Is the answer odd or even? Is the answer a multiple of 3?

3. $20 \times 3 \div 4 + 23 + 17 + 83 = $ _____. Is the answer odd or even? Is the answer a multiple of 5?

4. $234 \div 6 \times 2 + 103 = $ _____. Is the answer a multiple of 5? Divide the answer by 3. What is the final answer now?

5. $200 + 309 \times 25 \div 15 + 10 = $ _____. Is the answer a multiple of 5? Is the answer a multiple of 3?

6. Jennifer had 37 autographed baseballs, but she sent 29 to her older brother Harry, who missed playing baseball when he was away visiting a friend in France. If she doesn't get any new ones, how many autographed baseballs does she have left?

7. Taylor planted a patch of strawberries in his back-yard. In June they were beautiful, ripe, and ready to pick. He went out with a basket and filled it up with 25 strawberries. He filled this basket 3 times, until there were no more strawberries. How many strawberries did he pick? Remember to approximate first.

8. Sondra invited 11 friends to her birthday party, and her dad bought 26 ice cream sandwiches. If Sondra and her friends each got an equal number of ice cream sandwiches, how many did each of them get? Were there any left over?

9. Taylor carried 26 loads of books to the library for Ms. Greely, who lived down the street. Each load weighed 251 pounds! (He used a wheelbarrow.) How many pounds of books did Taylor carry?

10. Jennifer got $39 from each of her 14 relatives. Now, she wants to use the money to buy as many maps as possible (she's a real travel buff). Each map costs $15. How many maps can she buy, and will she have any money left over at the end?

Great job! You have mastered the basics. Now check out the answers and explanations, then see what Jennifer, Taylor, Sondra, and Beauregard are doing in the neighborhood.

Chapter 3
Fractions

When the pizza came out of the oven it was beautiful and steamy and smelled of tomatoes and garlic. Everyone was hopping around the kitchen because they couldn't wait to eat it.

"Okay," said Beauregard, who'd put on a big white mushroom-shaped chef's hat, "Step aside, step aside . . . it's time to add the mouse heads. Whoops! Only joking. Now, let's cut this thing."

Here's the first cut. He cut straight down the middle of the pizza, like this:

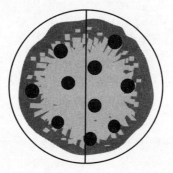

How much of the pizza is each piece? One-half, also known as $\frac{1}{2}$. This number is a **fraction**. A fraction is a number that is usually used to show a part of something bigger. Here is how you can tell that each piece of this pizza is one-half. The whole pizza, at this point in its life, is made up of two pieces. In a fraction you put the number that shows the whole thing on the bottom.

$$\overline{2} \leftarrow \text{Whole}$$

One piece of this pizza is one part, the number on the top of the fraction.

$$\frac{1}{2} \begin{array}{l} \leftarrow \text{Part} \\ \leftarrow \text{Whole} \end{array}$$

So a fraction shows what part of the whole you have. A piece is one part out of a possible two parts.

What if you had more parts than whole? Impossible? Not really—what if you had a whole pie cut into five equal pieces (or $\frac{5}{5}$) and an extra equal-sized slice. That would be $\frac{6}{5}$. You have more than the whole: this means your fraction is greater than 1. If you have fewer parts than the whole, say one part out of two, then the fraction is less than a whole, less than 1. (The line in the middle of a fraction, called the fraction bar, also means to divide. But we'll get to that later.)

THINK ABOUT THIS

$5 = \frac{5}{1}$, $3 = \frac{3}{1}$, $1 = \frac{1}{1}$, since you have 5 wholes, 3 wholes, etc. Any number can be written as a fraction by putting it over 1—that's because dividing by 1 doesn't change anything.

Beauregard made the next cut in the pizza and it looked like this.

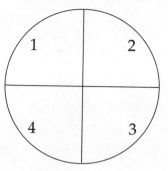

What would you call one of the pieces of the pizza as it is cut up now? How would you write it down? Like this: $\frac{1}{4}$. This is called one-fourth, or one-quarter. How did you know what the fraction looked like? Because the piece is one part out of a whole of four pieces. Fractions are part over whole.

What if you had two of these slices?

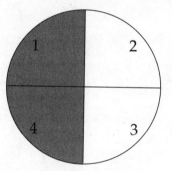

You would have $\frac{2}{4}$, or two-fourths. But what else does this look like? That's right, it looks an awful lot like one-half, from before. As you can see from the picture, $\frac{1}{2}$ and $\frac{2}{4}$ are equal.

How could you tell these fractions were equal if you didn't have a picture? By **reducing**. Reducing is a way of putting a fraction into its simplest form. How do you know $\frac{2}{4} = \frac{1}{2}$? Take a more careful look at $\frac{2}{4}$. The question to ask yourself is: can you divide the top and bottom numbers of the fraction by the same number? Well, are 2 and 4 divisible by the same number? Sure they are. Both 2 and 4 are even, so they are divisible by 2. So you will want to divide both the top and the bottom by 2:

$$\frac{2}{4} \begin{array}{c} \div \ 2 \\ \div \ 2 \end{array} = \frac{1}{2} \text{ so } \frac{2}{4} \text{ becomes } \frac{1}{2}.$$

Now, can 1 be divided into anything smaller? Nope, so this fraction is now in its most reduced form. Phew.

Let's try a few others.

$$\frac{3}{6}$$

Does $\frac{3}{6}$ have a number that divides evenly into the top and the bottom? Here's another way that knowing your times tables will come in handy. Both 3 and 6 are divisible by 3. $\frac{3}{6}$ divided top and bottom by 3 becomes $\frac{1}{2}$.

Do all fractions reduce to $\frac{1}{2}$? *No.* How about this one:

$$\frac{4}{16}$$

What number goes into both the top and the bottom? Well, let's try 2, because both top and bottom are even. $\frac{4}{16}$ divided top and bottom by 2 becomes $\frac{2}{8}$. Are you done yet? No, not yet, because 2 and 8 can both be divided again.

2 and 8 both divided by 2 give you $\frac{1}{4}$. Is this fraction in its most reduced form? Yes, because you cannot make the 1 any smaller. If you wanted to, you could have reduced the fraction by 4 and skipped a step.

$$\frac{4 \div 4 = 1}{16 \div 4 = 4}$$

This is not necessary, and in fact, it is sometimes easier just to go by twos and threes, in small steps, so as not to make mistakes. If you want to, however, you can reduce by larger numbers, as long as they are factors of both the top and the bottom of the fraction.

The spicy aroma of the freshly cut pizza filled the kitchen.

"I'm hungry as a horse," said Jennifer.

"I think I could use a nibble or two," said Sondra.

Taylor silently stared at the pizza as though he'd fallen in love.

"I guess we'd better finish cutting up this pie quickly," Beauregard exclaimed. He made two more rapid slices across the pizza. It looked like this:

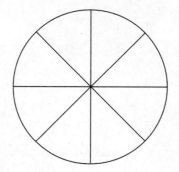

Everyone took a piece.

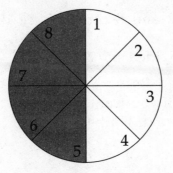

Beauregard ate his slice the way cats eat everything, cleanly and neatly, without getting so much as a smudge of tomato sauce on his whiskers. Taylor ate his slice slowly, with a look of dreamy satisfaction. Sondra put hers on a plate, carefully removed the crust, then cut the rest into tiny cheesy pieces that she ate with a fork. Jennifer, however, grabbed up her slice and wolfed it down so fast that before anyone else had noticed she was into her second piece.

The cat and the three kids had each had a slice of pizza, then Jennifer had grabbed another, so now the pizza was missing five pieces.

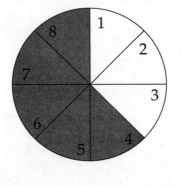

How would you write the full pizza out as a fraction? Well, there are 8 pieces, out of a whole of 8, so $\frac{8}{8}$. And how much is that? Well, it is the whole pizza, 1 whole pizza, so it is equal to 1. Any number over itself in a fraction is equal to 1. Really. You may remember the fraction bar from division.

$$\frac{8}{8} \leftarrow \text{bar}$$

A fraction bar means divide the top number by the bottom number, so if you had any doubts as to what $\frac{8}{8}$ was, ask yourself, "What is 8 divided by 8?" It is 1.

THINK ABOUT THIS

Since a fraction bar means divide, and you can never divide by 0, the bottom part of the fraction can *never* be 0.

How many pieces of pizza are in the process of being eaten? Five pieces. What fractional part of the pizza is being eaten? Well, 5 parts out of a whole of 8, so $\frac{5}{8}$ or five-eighths. So what part is left? Well, you can look at the picture and see 3 pieces left, which means 3 out of 8, so $\frac{3}{8}$ or three-eighths. Practice working with fractions. To find out how much is left, subtract what was eaten from the whole:

$$\frac{8}{8} - \frac{5}{8} =$$

The trick with subtracting fractions—and for adding them too—is that you only subtract or add the top part of the fraction. By the way, the top part of a fraction is called the **numerator**, and the bottom part of the fraction is called the **denominator**. So:

$$\frac{8}{8} - \frac{5}{8} = \frac{3}{8}$$

This is because the whole doesn't change, just the number of pieces taken or left changes.

How about if you combine what is left with what is being eaten?

$$\frac{3}{8} + \frac{5}{8} =$$

You add only the numerators (the tops).

$$\frac{3}{8} + \frac{5}{8} = \frac{8}{8} \text{ or } 1$$

✎ ✎ ✎ ✎ ✎

"This is the best pizza I've ever had!" Jennifer said between big, happy mouthfuls.

"Delicious, yes, but I believe I've had quite enough to satisfy my appetite," Beauregard commented.

"Mmmmm," Taylor nodded, "I hate to say it, but I'm feeling pretty good now, too."

"That was excellent," Sondra said, untucking the napkin she'd folded round her collar.

"Do you mean *I can have the rest?*" Jennifer cried, her eyes lighting up like the headlights on a car. "Eyaaa!" She dive-bombed the remaining pizza.

"Hit the deck!" Beauregard cried.

Sondra, Taylor, and Beauregard took cover under the kitchen table. Tomato sauce and cheese flew in all directions. When it was over, not more than a couple of seconds later, Jennifer sat smiling on the floor, patting her tummy amid a puddle of dripping cheese and tomato. "Excellent."

How much pizza did Jennifer eat? Let's see. She ate 2 pieces at first—or two-eighths—which is one-quarter of a pizza.

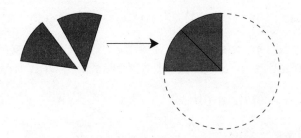

Then she ate the 3 pieces left over, or three-eighths. So how much is $\frac{1}{4} + \frac{3}{8}$? Well, we can also write this as $\frac{2}{8} + \frac{3}{8} = \frac{5}{8}$.

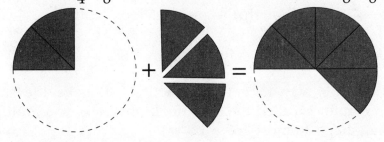

The great thing is, you always add fractions by making the denominators of the fractions the same. This is called forming a **common denominator**. A common denominator means the same denominator. There are two easy ways to make the denominators of fractions the same. The first way is what you just did.

$$\frac{3}{8} + \frac{1}{4} =$$

You saw that one of the denominators is a multiple of the other denominator. In this case, 2 times 4 is 8, so 8 is a multiple of 4. Multiply the top and bottom of the fraction $\frac{1}{4}$ by 2. 1 times 2 is 2. 2 times 2 is 4. Presto: $\frac{1}{4}$ turns into $\frac{2}{8}$.

Why does this work? Well, to make $\frac{1}{4}$ have a denominator of 8 you need to multiply the 4 by 2. But because you don't want to change the value of the fraction, you multiply the top by 2 as well, multiply $\frac{1}{4}$ by $\frac{2}{2}$. Why? Well, what is the value of $\frac{2}{2}$? Any number over itself equals 1: $\frac{2}{2}$ equals 1. What happens when you multiply a number by 1? Not a thing, the number stays the same. So when you multiply $\frac{1}{4}$ by $\frac{2}{2}$, even though the product looks different, $\frac{2}{8}$, the value of the number stays the same. So, $\frac{3}{8} + \frac{1}{4} = \frac{3}{8} + \frac{2}{8} = \frac{5}{8}$

The other way to get the fractions to have the same denominator is called the **bow tie**. In this case, you multiply in the shape (almost) of a bow tie.

$$\frac{3}{8} + \frac{1}{4} =$$

First, multiply up diagonally from the right to the left, and write the number over the left side:

Then multiply up diagonally from the left to the right, and write the number down above the right side.

$$\frac{3}{8} \nearrow^{8} + \frac{1}{4}$$

Then, multiply the two denominators and write that product as the denominator of your answer.

$$\frac{3}{8} + \frac{1}{4} = \overline{32}$$

Last, add the two floating numbers to form the numerator of your answer.

$$\frac{12 + 8}{\frac{3}{8} \times \frac{1}{4}} = \frac{12 + 8}{32} = \frac{20}{32}$$

Can you reduce $\frac{20}{32}$? Sure. First divide the top and the bottom by $\frac{2}{2}$.

$$\frac{20}{32} \div \frac{2}{2} = \frac{10}{16}$$

Can you reduce again? Sure.

$$\frac{10}{16} \div \frac{2}{2} = \frac{5}{8}$$

Ta da! No surprise, the same answer calculated in a slightly different way.

✎ ✎ ✎ ✎ ✎

Meanwhile, back in Beauregard's kitchen, Sondra was mighty annoyed with Jennifer.

"You ate more than half the pie!" Sondra yelled.

"I'm a growing girl," said Jennifer sheepishly.

"But there's none left for anyone else!"

"Well, you didn't want yours," said Jennifer.

"You assumed we didn't want any more. Maybe we wanted to save our pieces for later."

"Oh, I guess you're right, I'm sorry."

"Well, I'm sorry I yelled at you," Sondra said. "But look at the mess . . ."

"I got carried away. That pizza *was* pretty amazing. And I'll clean it up, okay?" Jennifer started wiping up the great blobs of tomato and cheese, but soon the others felt sorry for her and decided to help.

By the time they agreed to help, though, Jennifer had already cleaned up $\frac{1}{2}$ the room.

Here's how they divided the rest:

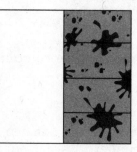

Jennifer

Sondra

Beauregard

Taylor

How much is left for Jennifer to clean? You can probably see that there's $\frac{1}{8}$ left for her to clean. Beauregard, Sondra, and Taylor each clean $\frac{1}{8}$, which is $\frac{3}{8}$ in total.

But what if you didn't have a diagram? How would you find out how much there was left for Jennifer to clean? Well, here's one way you could set up the problem:

$$\frac{1}{2} - \frac{3}{8} =$$

Now use the bow tie. You can use the bow tie for subtraction as well as addition. You do almost the exact same things. First, multiply up from right to left, and put the product over the left side.

$$\overset{8}{\underset{2}{\nwarrow}}\frac{1}{2}\searrow\frac{3}{8}$$

Then, multiply up from the left to the right and put the product over the right side.

$$\frac{1}{2}\nearrow\frac{3}{8}\overset{6}{\nearrow}$$

Then, multiply the denominators and put the product under the fraction bar as the new denominator.

$$\frac{1}{2} - \frac{3}{8} = \overline{16}$$

Now for the different part: instead of adding the two floating numbers, you subtract them! Not surprising, is it?

$$\overset{8 \quad - \quad 6}{\underset{2 \rightarrow 8}{\times}} = \frac{8-6}{16} = \frac{2}{16}$$

Can you reduce $\dfrac{2}{16}$? Sure.

$$\frac{2}{16} \div \frac{2}{2} = \frac{1}{8}$$

By the way, does any of this remind you of the pizza? It should, because Beauregard and the kids each cleaned the exact same **proportion** of the room as they ate of the pizza. Sondra, Taylor, and Beauregard each ate 1 slice, or $\dfrac{1}{8}$ of the pizza, and they each cleaned $\dfrac{1}{8}$ of the room. Jennifer ate $\dfrac{5}{8}$ of the pizza and she cleaned $\dfrac{5}{8}$ of the room.

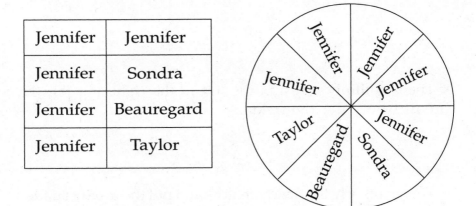

Jennifer	Jennifer
Jennifer	Sondra
Jennifer	Beauregard
Jennifer	Taylor

We aren't saying that the room and the pizza are the same size or shape or are equal in any way. What is equal is the *part* of the room cleaned by each kid, or cat, compared to the *part* of the pizza eaten by each one. If you read $\dfrac{1}{2}$ of a 100-page book (50 pages) and your friend reads $\dfrac{1}{2}$ of a 10-page book (5 pages), then you and your friend didn't read the same book or the same amount of pages, but you did read the exact same proportion of your books, $\frac{1}{2}$.

✎ ✎ ✎ ✎ ✎

When they were done cleaning, Beauregard said, "Now what about a little dessert?"

Sondra and Taylor shook their heads, but Jennifer looked interested, "What kind of dessert? Nothing with mice in it I hope."

"Mice? For *dessert*? That would be crazy. No, it just so happens I have a blueberry pie."

"Blueberry pie? That's my favorite," Sondra said.

"Me too," Taylor said.

"I like blueberry pie, somewhat," Jennifer said, trying to appear calm.

"Maybe I'll just have a teensy piece," Taylor said.

"Make mine extra teensy," Sondra said.

"Jennifer?" Beauregard inquired.

"Pie! Blueberry pie! I'll have a *whomping, huge piece* . . . I'll have . . ." Jennifer suddenly stopped, noticing her friends were looking at her strangely—"a medium sized, er, uh semi-small, or else small, better make my slice of pie very, very small, okay?" She thought for a second. "But I can have seconds, *right*?"

"Of course," Beauregard said. "If there's enough for everyone else too, and I'm sure there will be . . . but here, let me cut you a small slice."

"Oh that's too big," Jennifer almost choked as she did her best to be polite. She loved blueberry pie and could have easily eaten the whole thing.

"Would you rather have three-eighths of this slice, or two-ninths?"

"Um," said Jennifer. "Uh, er, well, I'll have to get back to you on that."

Poor Jennifer! She was trying so hard, at that point, she wasn't sure which one to pick. Which one would you choose?

One cool thing about the bow tie is that you can use it to tell which slice of pie is bigger. Take a look at $\frac{3}{8}$ and $\frac{2}{9}$. Just as you would if you were adding or subtracting these fractions, multiply up from both sides.

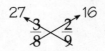

Whichever fraction is bigger will have the larger number above it. In this case, $\frac{3}{8}$ is bigger because it has 27 above it. Can you figure out why this works? It has to do with common denominators.

Beauregard and the kids sat around eating blueberry pie. Pretty soon they'd all eaten some pie and were feeling pretty good. How much blueberry pie do they have left? Well, between the four of them, they'd eaten $\frac{2}{8}$ of a pie. $\frac{8}{8}$ minus $\frac{2}{8}$ is $\frac{6}{8}$. So they have $\frac{6}{8}$ left. Can you reduce this fraction?

$$\frac{6 \div 2 = 3}{8 \div 2 = 4}$$

✎ ✎ ✎ ✎ ✎

Jennifer looked longingly at the remaining blueberry pie and inquired, "Does anybody mind if I have some more?"

"Go right ahead," Beauregard replied. " I've got another one in the refrigerator."

So they have $\frac{3}{4}$ of one pie plus another whole pie. There are several ways to write this. First, let's try it as one big fraction. The whole pie could be written $\frac{8}{8}$ (assuming we wanted to slice it into $\frac{1}{8}$ ths, which is a common way to slice a pie), and we'll use $\frac{6}{8}$ for the pie the kids have already started on, because this way we already have a common denominator.

$$\frac{8}{8} + \frac{6}{8} = \frac{14}{8}$$

Can you reduce $\frac{14}{8}$? Sure.

$$\frac{14 \div 2 = 7}{8 \div 2 = 4}$$

They have $\frac{7}{4}$ left. This could remind you that a positive fraction whose numerator is bigger than its denominator is greater than 1. A fraction greater than 1 is also called an **improper fraction**. But when people talk about numbers like this, they usually don't say "seven-fourths." Instead, they present the fraction as a **mixed number**. A mixed number is a number that is a combination of a whole number and a fraction. Most kids say their ages as mixed numbers, like "twelve and a half."

Here is how to make a fraction into a mixed number. The fraction bar means divide, so that is what you will do.

$$\frac{7}{4}$$

Divide 4 into 7.

$$7 \div 4$$

How many times does 4 go into 7? One, so that will be your whole number. The remainder is 3, and that will go over the denominator.

$$4\overline{)7}^{\,1R3}$$

$\frac{7}{4}$ is equal to $1\frac{3}{4}$.

If you ever want to convert an improper fraction to a mixed number, just divide and put the remainder over the denominator, next to the quotient.

Try it again.

$$\frac{7}{2}$$

Well, 2 goes into 7 three times, with a remainder of 1. The remainder goes over the denominator, which gives you $3\frac{1}{2}$.

To convert a mixed number into a fraction is easy, too. Let's try it with $4\frac{2}{3}$. Multiply the denominator by the whole number. Now, add that to the numerator.

$$4\frac{2}{3} = 4\frac{2}{3} = \frac{12+2}{3} = \frac{14}{3}$$

Then put the whole mess over the original denominator, and you get $\frac{14}{3}$. There you are, it's an improper fraction again.

Why would you want to convert mixed numbers into improper fractions? Because that's the easiest way to add and subtract them.

$$3\frac{2}{3} - 1\frac{1}{2} \text{ becomes } \frac{11}{3} - \frac{3}{2} =$$

Well, now you can use the bow tie, and if you feel like it you can convert the answer into a mixed number.

$$\overset{22}{\underset{3}{11}} \overset{9}{\underset{2}{3}} = \overset{13}{\underset{6}{}}$$

$\dfrac{13}{6}$ becomes $2\dfrac{1}{6}$.

✍ QUIZ #2 ✍
Fractions

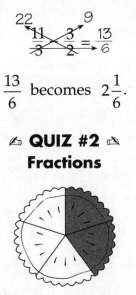

1. What fractional part of the pie is shaded?

2. What fractional part of the pie is shaded? Put this fraction in its most reduced form.

3. What fractional part of the pie is shaded? Combine it with the fraction of the pie in question 3 above, then put this final fraction in its most reduced form.

4. $3\dfrac{1}{2} - 1\dfrac{2}{5} =$

5. $9\dfrac{2}{3} + 1\dfrac{1}{2} =$

6. Rose has $\dfrac{1}{4}$ of an apple pie, and her friend has $\dfrac{2}{4}$ of the same pie. Together, Rose and her friend have what fractional part of the apple pie?

7. Lionel has $\dfrac{1}{4}$ of a bag of candy, his generous sister gives him $\dfrac{2}{4}$ of a bag of candy, and his mother, who doesn't know how much candy he already has or she wouldn't give it to him, gives him $\dfrac{1}{4}$ of a bag of candy. What fractional part of a bag of candy does Lionel have at the end of all this giving? Reduce.

8. Sondra had $\dfrac{6}{7}$ of a chocolate cake, and then her sister took $\dfrac{2}{5}$ of Sondra's part of the cake. What fractional part of the chocolate cake does Sondra have now, and do you think it is approximately more or less than $\dfrac{1}{2}$ the cake?

9. Taylor had 3 whole checker sets and $\dfrac{2}{3}$ of another. Then his uncle gave him 4 whole checker sets and $\dfrac{5}{6}$ of another. How many checker sets does Taylor end up with? Try to approximate first.

10. Jennifer bought $10\frac{3}{4}$ gallons of fake blood, to play some kind of terrible trick on her good friend Taylor. On her way to set up the trick she spilled $3\frac{7}{8}$ gallons of fake blood. How much blood did she have left? And, before you even start the problem, if she needed at least 6 gallons for the trick, can you estimate whether she has enough at the end of the spill?

✎ ✎ ✎ ✎ ✎

Back at the house. Beauregard lay curled up on the couch snoozing the way he likes to after a good meal. As for the kids, well, Taylor and Sondra were staring in amazement and horror at Jennifer.

Jennifer had polished off the rest of the first blueberry pie and was now chowing down on the second one. Every time it seemed like she had to be finished, that she couldn't possibly fit another single berry into her stomach, she looked at the pie and said, "Maybe just one more little slice."

And it was true, she *was* taking small slices. At first the pie had been cut up into $\frac{1}{8}$ size pieces, but Jennifer had insisted on cutting each of the $\frac{1}{8}$ pieces in half.

Another way to say this is that Jennifer was taking $\frac{1}{2}$ *of* $\frac{1}{8}$. Almost any time you see the word "of" in a math problem, it means you should multiply. Multiplying fractions is easier than adding or subtracting them. To multiply fractions, you just multiply the top and the bottom straight across. No common denominator needed! So, $\frac{1}{2}$ of $\frac{1}{8}$ becomes $\frac{1}{2} \times \frac{1}{8} = \frac{1}{16}$.

The 1 times 1 of the numerators becomes 1, and the 2 times 8 of the denominators becomes 16.

This "of" trick works even if one of the numbers isn't a fraction. For example, what is $\frac{1}{4}$ of 12?

$$\frac{1}{4} \times 12 =$$

To multiply a fraction by a whole number, it is probably easier at first to look at the whole number as a fraction.

$$\frac{1}{4} \times \frac{12}{1} =$$

Any whole number can be seen as a fraction, just itself over 1. Then multiply straight across, and reduce.

$$\frac{1}{4} \times \frac{12}{1} = \frac{12}{4} = \frac{6}{2} = \frac{3}{1} = 3$$

A great thing about multiplying is that you have access to an extremely cool tool: **cancellation**. Cancellation is a bit like reducing the fractions before you multiply them. To cancel, you try to find common factors in the diagonal parts of the two fractions being multiplied.

$$\frac{2}{3} \times \frac{9}{16} =$$

Look at the diagonals: Do 3 and 9 have any common factors? Sure, 3 is a factor of both of them. So divide both by 3, and cancel the numbers.

$$\frac{2}{{}_1\cancel{3}} \times \frac{\cancel{9}^3}{16}$$

Look at the other diagonal: Do 2 and 16 have any common factors? Sure, 2 is a factor if both of them. Divide by 2 and cancel the numbers.

$$\frac{{}^1\cancel{2}}{3} \times \frac{9}{\cancel{16}_8}$$

Now, multiply straight across.

$$\frac{\overset{1}{\cancel{2}}}{\underset{1}{\cancel{3}}} \times \frac{\overset{3}{\cancel{9}}}{\underset{8}{\cancel{16}}} = \frac{3}{8}$$

Of course it would have worked the other way, without cancellation, but then you would have had to reduce at the end.

To multiply mixed numbers, translate them into improper fractions.

$$3\frac{1}{2} \times 2\frac{1}{5} \text{ becomes } \frac{7}{2} \times \frac{11}{5} = \frac{77}{10} = 7\frac{7}{10}$$

✎ ✎ ✎ ✎ ✎

Jennifer was down to the last $\dfrac{3}{4}$ of the second pie, eating $\dfrac{1}{16}$ at a time.

Sondra whispered to Taylor, "How many more of those stupid little pieces is she going to eat?"

"How should I know?"

"How many *could* she eat, max?" Sondra asked.

Jennifer had just finished another slice. She patted her stomach and looked at the rest of the pie, "Maybe I'll just have one more skinny little piece."

"I think she's going to eat the rest."

"How many little slices is that?"

_____

Another way to ask Sondra's question is, "How many $\frac{1}{16}$ size slices are there in $\frac{3}{4}$ of a blueberry pie?" Whenever you are trying to figure out how many pieces something can be split into, you are dealing with a division problem. How does one divide a fraction?

To divide by a fraction, **invert** the dividing fraction (you know, flip it, stand it on its head) and multiply. Invert means turn upside down, so $\frac{1}{16}$ would become $\frac{16}{1}$, and $\frac{2}{1}$ would become $\frac{1}{2}$. The new fraction formed when a fraction is inverted is called the **reciprocal** (just a fancy word for a flipped fraction). So 16 is the reciprocal of $\frac{1}{16}$. Or you can say this lovely rhyme: When dividing don't ask why, just flip it over and multiply.

Really, though, does it ever make sense not to ask why? Do you know why inverting the fraction works? We'll show you after we figure out the answer to the problem how many $\frac{1}{16}$ slices are in $\frac{3}{4}$ of a pizza.

Since the $\frac{3}{4}$ is divided by the $\frac{1}{16}$, $\frac{1}{16}$ is the fraction that gets flipped. The problem becomes $\frac{3}{4} \times \frac{16}{1}$.

Now that it is a multiplication problem you can cancel if you want to, but, *never ever cancel when you have a division set up, only cancel when you have a multiplication set up.* Can you live with a rule like that? You'll have to.

So, $\frac{3}{4} \times \frac{16}{1}$ cancels to $\frac{3}{1} \times \frac{4}{1} = 12$

There are 12 slices of $\frac{1}{16}$ each that fit into $\frac{3}{4}$ of a pizza.

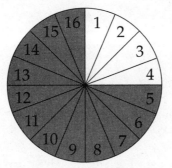

And of course, this works out just the same with mixed numbers. All you do is convert them to improper fractions before you start.

Have you figured out why you invert the fraction? Well, if you were going to divide 6 kids into 2 groups, how would you do it? You would divide 6 by 2. That can look like this $6 \div 2$, $2\overline{)6}$, or $\frac{6}{2}$. Look at that last one. Six over 2 is the same thing as $6 \times \frac{1}{2}$. So, to divide by 2, you actually multiply by $\frac{1}{2}$. Every time you divide you are merely multiplying by the number's reciprocal! Didn't know you had it in you, did you?

✍ QUIZ #3 ✍
Multiplying and Dividing Fractions

1. $\frac{1}{2} \times \frac{1}{3} =$

2. $\frac{2}{5} \times \frac{1}{9} =$

3. $\frac{1}{2} \div \frac{1}{2} =$

4. $3\dfrac{1}{2} \times \dfrac{2}{3} =$

5. $3\dfrac{1}{3} \div 5\dfrac{2}{9} =$

6. Beauregard has 6 bags of marbles. If he wants to give away $\dfrac{4}{5}$ of them, how many bags will he give away? (Put your answer in the form of a mixed number, it will be easier to understand that way.)

7. Sondra has $\dfrac{7}{8}$ of a pizza. How many skinny little $\dfrac{1}{32}$ slices are there in her $\dfrac{7}{8}$?

8. Taylor has $\dfrac{1}{5}$ of an apple, and he wants to give his brother $\dfrac{1}{3}$ of it. How much of the apple is Taylor going to give his brother?

9. Taylor and Jennifer have $3\dfrac{1}{2}$ cantaloupes. Jennifer is going on a picnic and she wants to take one-fifth of their cantaloupe stash with her. How much cantaloupe will she take? Will it even be one whole cantaloupe? Can you approximate before you do the problem?

10. Jennifer has a bug collection that consists of $5\dfrac{3}{5}$ bags of bugs. How many $\dfrac{1}{4}$ bags of bugs does she have in her collection?

Taylor and Sondra gaped at Jennifer. There was just one more tiny piece of pie left.

"She can't do it," Taylor whispered. "No way."

"It makes my stomach hurt just to watch," Sondra said.

Jennifer pushed her chair back from the table and groaned, "I am absolutely, completely, and totally stuffed." She stood up unsteadily, holding on to the back of the chair. Oh, but then she looked back at the pie.

And the pie looked at Jennifer. Okay, it didn't *really* look, but to Jennifer the pie seemed to stare right into her with soft blueberry eyes and say, "Please! Don't leave me! Eat me too! I taste as good as the other pieces . . . You can't abandon me like this after I've waited so long . . . please Jennifer, *pleeeeaaaaaaasssssssssseeeeeeeeee.*"

Jennifer flopped back into the chair. "Maybe I'll have just this one more teeny-tiny piece of pie."

✍ QUIZ #4 ✍
Review

1. Which 2 of the following 5 numbers are equal?

$$\frac{1}{5} \quad \frac{3}{6} \quad \frac{2}{3} \quad \frac{1}{2} \quad \frac{4}{10}$$

2. $\dfrac{1}{2} + \dfrac{1}{3} =$

3. $\dfrac{3}{4} \div \dfrac{2}{3} =$

4. $\dfrac{3}{8} \times 3\dfrac{2}{3} =$

5. $3\dfrac{1}{2} \div 5\dfrac{1}{2} =$

6. Rose has $\frac{2}{3}$ of a pizza pie. Is that the same as if she had $\frac{3}{6}$ of a pizza pie?

7. Taylor has $\frac{1}{2}$ of a box of dominoes. Taylor's friend says, "I want $\frac{1}{3}$ of those dominoes," and Taylor says, "Okay." If Taylor gives his friend what he asks for, what part of the box of dominoes will Taylor give away?

8. Sondra has $3\frac{3}{8}$ gallons of crazy glue. If fixing a certain statue only uses $\frac{1}{4}$ of the crazy glue, how much glue will the repair use? And, how much glue will she have left?

9. Taylor has $2\frac{2}{3}$ buckets of nails, but the nails are really heavy, so he wants to put them into buckets that are filled up only $\frac{1}{4}$ of the way. How many 1/4 full buckets could he separate his nails into?

10. Jennifer has $5\frac{3}{4}$ bags of hair. If she was able to sell $\frac{3}{8}$ of the hair to a farmer to scare away deer, how much of the hair is she left with?

Terrific. You are officially a fraction superstar. So, onward and upward to the next math challenge.

Chapter 4
Decimals

Sondra, Taylor, and Beauregard watched in amazement as Jennifer swallowed the last bite of the last piece of pie.

"She did it," Beauregard said. Sondra and Taylor nodded solemnly.

At last Jennifer pushed herself away from the table and its empty plates. "Uh-boy, I don't feel so good."

"She's going to barf. Definitely," Taylor said.

"You are *so gross*, Taylor," Sondra said quietly, because it really did look as if Jennifer might be sick.

"I am not gross," Taylor said, "my *ideas* are gross." Then he added, "Besides, if you think I'm gross wait until Jennifer tosses up *pizza and blueberries. That's* gross!"

"Ubf," Jennifer gulped.

"Pardon?" said Beauregard.

"Erpf-ubf," went Jennifer.

"She's gonna really blow chunks," Taylor noted appreciatively.

"Glrbff-erpf-ubf- GLRBFF GL-R-BF-F . . ." Jennifer sounded bad but she looked worse. She staggered around Beauregard's tiny kitchen clutching her stomach.

"Heavens. Maybe she's just going to cough up a hairball. That happens to us cats from time to time. Oh my heavens . . . "

Suddenly Jennifer froze in place. Her eyes bugged out like

Ping-Pong balls. She stopped right in front of Taylor and turned toward him. Her mouth flung open—wide, gaping.

"Fake out!" Jennifer screamed. "You're *busted*."

Taylor looked green. Sondra and Beauregard let out their breath. They were too stunned to laugh very hard, but they did manage to chuckle.

"Ah, I feel great. There's nothing like a nice big meal to make my day."

"You're crazy," Taylor said hotly.

"I'm not crazy," Jennifer said, "my *ideas* are crazy."

Even Taylor laughed at that.

For a little while the three kids and Beauregard amused themselves repeating the scene. Sondra imitated the face Taylor made when Jennifer stopped in front of him. Beauregard imitated the way Jennifer staggered and held her stomach. And Taylor imitated what he thought he was going to look like, standing there covered in blueberry-pizza stomach slime. They were having a really good time until Sondra said:

"Is it getting warmish in here?"

It *was* getting warm in Beauregard's house. And humid. Mushy even.

"I think the air-conditioner has broken down. I don't hear it any more," Taylor said.

It was true. The air-conditioner had broken down. Beauregard tried unplugging it and plugging it back in, but it was no use. Now that they'd noticed it, Beauregard's tiny house began to feel very hot indeed. It felt like an oven. A damp oven.

"I feel like I'm standing in somebody's mouth," Taylor said. "Well, at least they don't have bad breath and I'm not threatened by blueberry pizza mush."

"We should go out," Sondra suggested.

"Yeah, but where?" Jennifer said.

"Oh well, I think it's perfectly comfortable," Beauregard said, "*and* I'm wearing fur. But I'll do what the group decides."

"Hey, the movies are air-conditioned," Sondra said.

"Excellent, the movies. Good thinking," Jennifer agreed.

"Yeah, but who's going to pay?" Taylor said. "I don't think I have the cash."

"Let's pool our resources and see how close we are," Jennifer said.

The kids searched their pockets. Beauregard searched among the cushions on the couch.

"I've got five dollars and twenty-three cents," Sondra said.

"I've got one dollar and twenty-nine cents," said Jennifer.

"I've got sixty-seven cents," said Taylor.

"Well look here," Beauregard said, poking in the couch, "so far I've found four cents."

5.23   1.29   0.67   0.04

Do you recognize these types of numbers? Sure, because almost all money is written out this way. These numbers are called decimals. Decimals are another type of fraction.

Sondra has five dollars and twenty-three cents; this is written in number form as 5.23 (we're leaving out the dollar sign because the things we're writing about apply to all numbers written in this form, not just American money). The whole in this case is a dollar. Sondra has 5 whole dollars, and 0.23 parts of another dollar. What is another way of looking at 0.23? $\frac{23}{100}$.

Did you ever think about why pennies are called "cents"? The root "cents" is part of the word **cent**ury, and bi**cent**ennial. It means one hundred. There are 100 cents in a dollar, so each cent or penny, is $\frac{1}{100}$ of a dollar. And 23 cents are $\frac{23}{100}$ of a dollar.

THINK ABOUT THIS

Decimals that don't have whole numbers—for example, if you have only cents and no whole dollars—are almost always written with a zero in the ones place. Why? Maybe someone just didn't want decimals less than 1 to look lonely.

The important thing about decimals is the **decimal point**. The decimal point is that dot to the right of the units digit.

$$5.23$$

Do you remember digits places? Well, there are even more digits places than you might have thought. The place directly to the right of the decimal point is called the **tenths** place.

$$5.23$$
tenths

This shows two-tenths, or $\frac{2}{10}$. That's why we have dimes; dimes are tenths of dollars.

To the right of the tenths place is the hundredths place.

$$5.23$$
hundredths

This shows there are three one-hundredths, or $\frac{3}{100}$, better known in dollar form as three cents. Altogether, it is twenty-three one hundredths, better known as twenty-three cents.

To read the whole number aloud as a decimal, say "five point two three."

"Let's see," Jennifer said, "approximately how much do we have altogether? I have about a dollar and thirty cents, Sondra has about five dollars and a quarter, Taylor has about seventy cents, and Beauregard is basically broke."

"That hardly seems fair," Beauregard said. "I'm not broke, I have four pennies, shiny ones at that."

"No offense, Beau. I was just rounding off!"

How did Jennifer approximate all of those numbers? Did you approximate as you were reading? One way to make approximating easier is to **round**. Rounding means taking numbers and getting rid of their smaller, less important parts. If you were some big business executive and you were trying to figure out how much it would cost you to buy fifty buildings, you probably wouldn't come up with a number like 5 million and 10 dollars and 14 cents. The 10 dollars and 14 cents would get rounded off, and you would say, "These buildings cost about 5 million dollars."

Here is how to round. First, find out to what digit place you are rounding. Suppose you wanted to round to the tens place. We will round 234 to the tens place. Notice, that is *tens* not *tenths*. Here is the tens place on a number:

$$234$$
↑
tens

To round, look at the number directly to the right of the place to which you are rounding. If that number is 5 or above, add one to the number to the left. If the number to the right of the place on which you are rounding is below 5, leave the number to the left as is, and replace the numbers to the right with 0.

So, if you are rounding 234 to the tens place, the digit to the right of the tens place is 4. Is 4 larger or smaller than 5? Smaller, so the digit to the left, 3, will stay the same. 234 becomes 230.

Take a look at a number line.

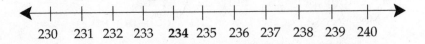

Which is 234 closer to, 230 or 240? The number line shows you that 234 is closer to 230.

Try again. Round 3,761 to the hundreds place. Which is the hundreds place? Where the 7 is. First, look to the number to the right of the 7. It is larger than 5, so the 7 becomes an 8. Then, the 6 and the 1, all the numbers to the right, disappear.

3,761 becomes 3,800.

To see this more clearly, look at a number line.

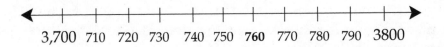

Which hundred is 3,761 closer to, the 3,800 or the 3,700? The number line is a great way to see how rounding works.

Decimals round the same way. Try rounding 34.12 to the *tenths* place. Where is the tenths place? Just to the right of the decimal point, in this case, where the 1 is. The number to the right of the tens place is 2. Is 2 greater or less than 5? Less, so the 1 stays the same and the numbers to the right of it disappear. 34.12 becomes 34.1 (or 34.10 if you still want it to look like money). The decimal isn't affected by the 0 the way a whole number would be.

THINK ABOUT THIS

A 0 at the end of a decimal doesn't affect that decimal's value. Why? Think about how decimals look when they are fractions. 0.5 is really $\frac{5}{10}$ and 0.50 is really $\frac{5}{100}$. Can you reduce these?

$$\frac{5}{10} \div \frac{5}{5} = \frac{1}{2} \quad \text{and} \quad \frac{50}{100} \div \frac{10}{10} = \frac{5}{10} \div \frac{5}{5} = \frac{1}{2}$$

Reduced, they are the same, you could add on ten trillion zeroes to the right of a decimal and it wouldn't make a speck of difference.

✎ ✎ ✎ ✎ ✎

"I've got five dollars and twenty-three cents," said Sondra. So, 5.23, if we are rounding to the nearest tenth, becomes 5.20.

"I've got sixty-seven cents," said Taylor. So 0.67 rounded to the nearest tenth becomes 0.70.

"I've got one dollar and twenty-nine cents," Jennifer said. So 1.29 becomes 1.30.

"I have four cents," said Beauregard. Well, 0.04 becomes 0.00, because four is smaller than five so it disappears.

"Well," said Jennifer, after a few quick calculations with paper and pencil, "I'd say we have a little more than seven dollars."

How did Jennifer calculate that there was about seven dollars altogether? By adding the rounded decimals. Since decimals are another type of fraction, the way to add them will not surprise you: You need a common denominator. What may surprise you is that a common denominator for decimals only means *line up the decimals according to their places.*

This:
$$\begin{array}{r} 2.3 \\ +3. \\ \hline \end{array}$$

Not this: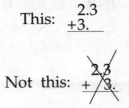

Can you figure out how this works? Well, what would the denominators of all the numbers in the hundredths place be if they were fractions? That's right, hundredths means denominators of 100. And the tenths place has denominators of 10. Decimals can even go further to the right, to the **thousandths place**, and beyond.

$$0.052$$
$$\uparrow$$
thousandths

When these numbers are lined up, everything in the same decimal place has the same denominator, and you can just add.

Try it with the rounded numbers that Jennifer added:

$$\begin{array}{r} 5.20 \\ 0.70 \\ 1.30 \\ \underline{0.10} \\ = 7.30 \end{array}$$

which she then rounded off to about seven dollars.

How would the unrounded numbers add up?

$$\begin{array}{r} 5.23 \\ 0.67 \\ 1.29 \\ \underline{0.04} \\ = 7.23 \end{array}$$

Rounding worked pretty well as an approximating tool, didn't it?

Subtracting decimals works the same way. Just line up the decimal places and subtract as you would any number.

$$
\begin{array}{rcr}
3.05 & & 3.05 \\
-\ \underline{2.2\ } & \text{becomes} & \underline{2.20} \\
& & =0.85
\end{array}
$$

As you can see here, if you have a number without a digit in one of the decimal places, you can just add a 0 to make it less confusing. This is most helpful when you subtract.

✍ QUIZ #5 ✍
Decimals

1. Round 234 to the nearest hundred.

2. Round 13.45 to the nearest tenth.

3. Round 2.34 and 3.45 to the nearest tenth, then add the two rounded numbers.

4. $10.879 - 7.345 =$

5. $12.3 + 7.52 =$

6. Sondra has 2 dollars and 32 cents. Which number occupies the tenths place?

7. Taylor has 3 dollars and 79 cents, and he washes his uncle's car and earns 2 dollars and 50 cents. How much money does Taylor have at the end?

8. Sondra has 2 dollars and 32 cents, and she gives away 1 dollar and 98 cents. How much money does she have left? Now, express it as a fractional part of 1 dollar.

9. Taylor has 2.3537 grams of gold, and he is going to buy 0.0023 grams more tomorrow. How much gold will he have tomorrow after his purchase?

10. Jennifer had 4.3 gallons of cement, and she used 2.78 gallons to build a small fortress (very small). How much cement does she have left? Don't forget to approximate first.

"Seven dollars and change," Jennifer said, "not a whole heck of a lot."

"No good at all," said Sondra. Beauregard glumly shook his head.

"That's only enough for one of us to get into the movies," Taylor complained. But suddenly his expression changed, and a wicked glint flashed across his usually solemn eyes. "Of course, if *one* of us got in, that one of us, I'm not saying who—*Beauregard*—could slink past the ushers with cat-like stealth and hold the fire-exit doors open and get us into an air-conditioned movie for free!" Then Taylor's expression changed again dramatically. His mouth dropped at the corners and his eyes took on a bewildered, doomed-forever kind of look. "But then with my luck some crummy little usher would spot us because I'd step on a noisy candy wrapper left behind by some slob, at which point Jennifer would take off, and when Jennifer runs nobody can catch her. That would leave Sondra, Beauregard, and me. Sondra would talk her way out of it because she'd act so nice the usher would never believe she'd do something like sneak into the movies. Then there's Beauregard. Who's going to prosecute a cat? Nobody! And that leaves just me, as usual."

"Oh my God, Taylor, are you finished yet?" Sondra interrupted.

"Finished? *Finished*? I'll say I'd be finished! Who'd end up taking the fall? Me. Taylor. Mr. Fall Guy. But that's no big deal, you say. I mean we're only talking about sneaking into the movies; that's not a federal offense or anything. The usher'd only give me a warning, a "stern reprimand." That's how those people talk. But what would really happen is that somehow my mother would find out, she always finds out, and she'd treat me differently, and the kids in school too, they'd treat me differently. I'd become identified with crime, labeled a juvenile delinquent. I'd have begun my slow, unstoppable turn toward a life of crime—just another victim of the streets! And I'm only twelve! I'm too young, I tell ya! Too young! This whole idea of sneaking into the movies stinks! I don't like it. It's a set-up. A frame job. I won't do it. I just won't do it. We'll have to think of something else."

"Well, it's a good thing that's settled." Beauregard sighed with relief.

"Hey, I've got an idea," Sondra said. "Lemonade. Let's earn the money we need selling lemonade. On a hot day like this we ought to be able to make a fortune."

"Right," said Taylor. "First thing we've gotta do is *steal some lemons*. Okay, I'll drive the getaway bike . . ."

"Shut up!" the others yelled at him.

"Sondra, how much lemonade are we going to have to sell?" Jennifer wanted to know.

"Now that's a good question. There's four of us and it costs six dollars a ticket to get into the movies. That's $6.00 x 4, which is $24.00."

"Well, we've already got around $7.00. That's a start," Taylor said.

"No, we can forget about the $7.00 because it's going to cost that much to *buy* ingredients for the lemonade. Here's what we'll do. We'll make a fine, high-quality lemonade—Beauregard's Black-Cat Gourmet Lemonade—and sell it for $0.75 a glass."

Sounds like Sondra has a plan. How much money would the kids earn if they sold just 3 cups of lemonade? Seventy-five cents times 3. To do the problem you need to multiply decimals. To multiply decimals, simply set up an ordinary multiplication problem, like so:

$$\begin{array}{r} 0.75 \\ \times\ 3 \\ \hline \end{array}$$

You don't have to align the decimal point as with addition or subtraction. Just multiply as though the decimal point wasn't even there:

$$\begin{array}{r} 0.75 \\ \times\ 3 \\ \hline 225 \end{array}$$

Next, count the number of decimal places in the numbers you multiplied and, starting on the right of your product (225 in this case), count that number of decimal places over to the left. In this case, there are two spaces to the right of the decimal point in 0.75 and none in 3, so you start at the right of 225, and count over two decimal points to the left. 225 becomes 2.25.

$$225. \longrightarrow 2.25$$

So, $0.75 \times 3 = 2.25$. If the kids sold 3 cups of lemonade for 75 cents each, they'd have made $2.25.

When you multiply decimals by other decimals, add all the spaces to the right of the decimal points and use those. $0.5 \times 0.2 = 0.10$, because $5 \times 2 = 10$, then the decimal moves two to the left, one for each decimal place.

Now, let's say, excited by the money they were making, the kids decided to split up their income into five parts. One part each for Sondra, Taylor, Jennifer, and Beauregard, and one extra part for buying more ingredients to keep the lemonade business going. How would you figure this out? By dividing 2.25 by 5. Here is how the division problem would look.

$$5\overline{)2.25}$$

To divide a decimal by a whole number, simply put the decimal point on top of the roof-type thing. Then divide as you normally would, leaving the decimal point where it is.

$$
\begin{array}{r}
.45 \\
5{\overline{\smash{\big)}\,2.25}} \\
-20 \\
\hline
25 \\
25 \\
\hline
0
\end{array}
$$

Not too terrible.

How about dividing decimals by other decimals? Divide, for example, 2.5 by 0.5. First, set up your division.

$$0.5{\overline{\smash{\big)}\,2.5}}$$

Then, the number you are dividing by, in this case 0.5, needs to be altered so it looks like a whole number. So move the decimal point over to the right until it is a whole number. In this case, that means move the decimal point one space to the right. Then you must move the decimal point in the number being divided over the same number of spaces. In this case, move the decimal point one space to the right.

$$.5{\overline{\smash{\big)}\,2.5}} \longrightarrow 5{\overline{\smash{\big)}\,25}}$$

Then, divide normally.

$$25 \div 5 = 5$$

What if you divide into a whole number? Well, you still move the decimal point. Whole numbers have decimal points, they just aren't usually visible.

$$.5{\overline{\smash{\big)}\,30}} \longrightarrow 5{\overline{\smash{\big)}\,300.}}$$

$$5{\overline{\smash{\big)}\,300}} = 60$$

How do you think this works ? Well, a decimal is a fraction, right? So look at 0.5 as a fraction, then reduce.

$$0.5 = \frac{5}{10} = \frac{1}{2}$$

To divide by $\frac{1}{2}$, you actually multiply by $\frac{2}{1}$, remember?

$0.5\overline{)30}$ becomes $30 \div 0.5$ becomes $30 \div \frac{1}{2}$ becomes $30 \times \frac{2}{1} = 60$.

THINK ABOUT THIS

Sometimes it is much simpler to set decimal division up as fractions first. For instance, $0.57 \div 0.01$ may look confusing, but you can set it up first as a fraction $\frac{0.57}{0.01}$. Then move the decimal points on both the top and bottom halves the same number of places. Thus, $\frac{0.57}{0.01}$ is actually $\frac{57}{1}$.

$$\frac{0.57}{0.01} \longrightarrow \frac{57}{1}$$

and you know that any number divided by 1 is still the same number. Cool, huh?

You can also look at regular old division as decimals. For instance, $\frac{5}{10}$ is not only $\frac{1}{2}$, but also $5 \div 10$. Remember, the fraction bar means divide. Put the decimal place on top of the roof and you have

$$10\overline{)5.0}^{\,0.5}$$

Multiplying and Dividing Decimals

1. $2.3 \times 4 =$

2. $3.4 \div 2 =$

3. $2.1 \times 3.2 =$

4. $1.8 \div 0.9 =$

5. $2.3 \div 0.01 =$

6. If Taylor gets 3 dollars and 40 cents every time he empties his piggy bank, how much money will he have after he empties his piggy bank 4 times?

7. If Taylor has 5.2 ounces of snot captured in a tissue (gross) and he separates it (grosser) into two tissues that hold equal amounts, how many ounces of snot will each of the two tissues hold?

8. Taylor and Jennifer together have 7 dollars and they wanted to divide it into groups of 50 cents each, how many groups of 50 cents each would they have? Can you approximate this first?

9. Jennifer receives 3.02 pounds of Jell-O every time she knocks out the clown in the neighborhood carnival. If she knocks the clown out 2.5 times on an average day, how many pounds of Jell-O does she get on an average day? Remember to approximate first.

10. Jennifer has 0.45 ounces of fake blood in a glass, and she wants to separate it into glasses which each hold 0.05 ounces of fake blood. How many of these teeny tiny glasses will she need? How many do you approximate she will need?

YET ANOTHER THING TO THINK ABOUT

You already know that to multiply by 10 or a power of 10, you add a 0 onto the number. For instance, $3 \times 10 = 30$. What you are actually doing there is moving the decimal point to the right. When you divide by a power of 10, move the decimal point to the left.

$3,000 \div 10 = 300$. You can do this when dividing by decimals such as 0.01 as well. To divide by 0.01 is to divide by $\dfrac{1}{100}$, which means to multiply by 100, which means to move the decimal point two to the right. You don't always have to think of it exactly this way, but it is nice to know the connection is there, isn't it?

✍ QUIZ #7 ✍
Review

1. $2.3 + 4 =$

2. $3.5 - 2.7 =$

3. $1.2 \times 4 =$

4. $3.2 \div 2 =$

5. $2.4 \div 0.6 =$

6. Jennifer has 45 cents, and she gets 2 dollars and 55 cents for her birthday. How much money does she have altogether?

7. Taylor had 3 dollars and 15 cents, and he spent 1 dollar and 27 cents on a new box of tissues. How much is he left with?

8. For each basket Sondra makes at a charity basketball game, Barbara the bike-store owner donates 35 cents to the charity. If Sondra makes 6 baskets, how much money will Barbara donate to the charity? Can you approximate first?

9. Taylor receives 2.3 grams of lead every time he does a favor for his alchemy teacher. If he does 5 favors, how many grams of lead will he receive? Express your answer as a mixed number.

10. Jennifer wants to divide her 6.35 ounces of feathers into piles containing 0.5 ounces of feathers each. How many piles will there be at the end of the separation?

Terrific. Now, onwards to see where decimals can lead you.

Chapter 5
Ratios and Percentages

Beauregard brought out a gigantic fan. The three kids and the cat flopped on the floor of the living room in front of the fan to plan their lemonade empire.

"Do you think it is even possible to make enough money from lemonade to get into the movies?" Jennifer asked.

"No, it's bound to fail, fail miserably," Taylor groaned.

"Possible?" said Sondra, "It's way more than possible. From my preliminary calculations I'd say it's a sure thing. Figure seventy-five cents a cup. Okay, that's $0.75, so say we sell ten cups of lemonade. That's $7.50, which is $6.00 for the ticket with $1.50 left over to buy popcorn, soda, candy, whatever."

"Popcorn! Now you're really talking!" Jennifer cried enthusiastically.

"But," said Beauregard, "that's only $7.50. We have almost that much already."

Sondra raised a hand authoritatively, "Hold on, guys. All I was saying is we need to sell about ten cups of lemonade *for every one of us.*

"See," Taylor said, "I told you. It's no use. Let's be sensible and just accept our wretched, sweaty fate."

"I think we can do it," Sondra said.

"Well, we *do* still have to make the lemonade," Beauregard reminded them. "But I've got some good news, we're seven dollars and thirty cents ahead of schedule, because we don't

have to buy the ingredients. I've got all the fixings right here, including a lemonade recipe passed down to me by my great—and very beautiful—Aunt Georgette, a southern belle through and through, an exquisite lady, and a very fine hostess. I remember well sipping juleps and lemonade beneath the magnolias at her 'cottage.' That's what Aunt Georgette called her eighteen-room mansion. Goodness, it was at one of Aunt Georgette's soirees that I met little Miss Lola . . . a gray angora who wore the most fetching tiny pink bows in her hair. Ahhh, Lola . . . oh, but I digress . . . Here it is. Here's the recipe." Beauregard pulled out a piece of fine stationery, on which was written—in purple ink with wild, spiraling, curling, old-fashioned handwriting— the following recipe:

Lemonade

Cool fresh water

Fresh-squeezed lemon juice

Sugar

Combine water and sugar to form a thin syrup, then add lemon juice. Mix to taste. Serve in the shade of magnolias in bloom, from a crystal decanter, with ice cubes jingling against the glass like sleigh bells in summer.

"I'm a little worried about this recipe," said Taylor. "It isn't very clear, is it? What does mix to taste mean?"

"Well," said Jennifer, "we can taste test. Everyone knows that taste tests are the way the great chefs create masterpieces."

"We're doomed," Taylor said cheerfully.

"Relax, we're on our way to the movies," said Sondra.

Everybody rummaged around the kitchen searching for lemons and sugar. They cut up the lemons, squeezed out the juice (and picked out all the seeds), and made one batch as a taste test, using a formula of eight tablespoons of water to one tablespoon of lemon juice to three tablespoons of sugar. It looked wonderful, pale yellow and icy, and everybody stirred it ceremoniously with a long wooden spoon.

Then Jennifer (who else?) volunteered to be the taster. She dipped in the wooden spoon and took a sip. "Yuck! This is disgusting!

"The lemons were probably poisoned and you don't have long to live," Taylor said thoughtfully. "Oh well, it serves you right for eating all that pie."

"Yeah, and I'm taking you with me," Jennifer glared, making a fist.

"Come on, come on," Sondra said. "I'll bet the lemon to sugar ratio is off. Let's add some sugar."

When you make lemonade, or any other kind of mixture, you are dealing with a **ratio**. Ratios tell you the relative amounts in a mixture, for instance 8 tablespoons water to 1 tablespoon lemon juice to 3 tablespoons sugar is a ratio. You can express the ratio of water to lemon juice to sugar in either of these ways, 8:1:3, or 8 to 1 to 3. Both ways are said out loud as, "Eight to one to three." In a ratio, adding up the parts will give you the whole, as long as the measurement units are the same. In the lemonade recipe everything is given in tablespoons, so if the mixture has water, lemon juice, and sugar in a ratio of 8:1:3, then the whole of the mixture has 8 + 1 + 3 tablespoons, or 12 tablespoons.

Since this recipe says to combine the sugar and water to form a syrup and then add the lemon juice, we can look at the ratio between the syrup and the lemon juice. You have 1 tablespoon of lemon juice, and 11 tablespoons syrup. This ratio can be expressed in a number of ways. 1: 11, 1 to 11, or $\frac{1}{11}$. Look at that last version. You can't express a ratio with more than 2 parts this way, and it looks like a fraction. But it isn't a fraction, it's a ratio. A fraction would give $\frac{part}{whole}$. A ratio gives $\frac{part}{part}$. To get the whole, you have to add up the parts, 11 + 1 = 12. If you wanted to show the fractional part of the lemonade that was lemon juice, you would write $\frac{1}{12}$, $\frac{part}{whole}$. But $\frac{1}{11}$ is the ratio showing $\frac{part}{part}$.

Something to keep an eye on in ratios is the order of the parts. If you want the ratio of syrup to lemon juice, it is 11:1, but the ratio of lemon juice to syrup is 1:11. Stay on your toes and keep an eye out for which part comes first.

Ratios can be reduced, just like fractions. Ratios tell you what relative amounts are in a mixture. So if you make 1 million gallons of lemonade or just 1 glass, the ratio stays the same. Or if you have fruit punch instead of lemonade. For instance, if you have a ratio of $\frac{4}{6}$, 4 parts grape juice to 6 parts apple juice in punch, you can reduce the ratio as if it were a fraction.

$$\frac{4}{6} \div \frac{2}{2} = \frac{2}{3}$$

The ratio 2 to 3 is the same as the ratio of 4 to 6, because for every 2 parts of grape juice there will always be 3 parts of apple juice. And if the ratio is 2 to 3, it will always be 2 to 3, whether you have 5 gallons of punch, 5 teeny tiny cups of punch, or 5 million tanker trucks full of punch.

✎ ✎ ✎ ✎ ✎

"Just add one tablespoon of sugar and it will be much better," said Jennifer.

"Make sure you write it down!" said Sondra. "If we end up making the best lemonade in the world and don't have the recipe, that would really be a tragedy. You guys get the lemonade right while Beauregard and I withdraw to the living room to work out our marketing strategy."

"Who made her the boss?" Taylor grumbled after Sondra had left. Then he got a pad and paper and wrote: original—eight water, three sugar, one lemon juice. New—eight water, four sugar, one lemon juice.

"How is it now?" he asked.

Jennifer swished it around in her mouth and swallowed. "Almost perfect. Let's use one more tablespoon of lemon juice."

They mixed up a new batch, and Jennifer tasted it. She pronounced it absolutely perfect. " So what does that make the final recipe?" she asked.

"Well, eight tablespoons water, four tablespoons sugar, and two tablespoons lemon juice. So, eight to four to two. And the ratio of the syrup part to the lemon juice is twelve to two."

"So we have fourteen total tablespoons of lemonade? But we only have ten tablespoons of lemon juice to work with here, how much syrup will we need to make lemonade from that?"

When you use a ratio to figure out how much lemonade you will need for 1 million gallons, you actually use **proportion**. Proportions are the way you increase ratios. The ratio of syrup to lemon juice is 12 to 2, or $\frac{12}{2}$. To figure out how much you will need, set up the ratio next to the ratio you want, including the missing piece.

$$\frac{12}{2} = \frac{?}{10}$$

Since you know the ratios will always be equal, you are looking for a top part that will make that second ratio equal to $\frac{12}{2}$. The way to do this is to figure out what you multiplied the 2 by to get 10, then to multiply the top by that. Because you only multiply the ratio by some number over itself, which always equals 1, the ratio stays the same. See how the same things keep coming up?

To find the missing piece, multiply in two diagonals.

$$\frac{12}{2} \times \frac{?}{10} \qquad 120 = 2 \text{ times something}$$

120   ?

This is called **cross-multiplying**. You end up with $120 = 2 \times ?$ So 2 times the missing piece is 120. Now, to find out what the missing piece is you divide by 2. So, $120 \div 2 = 60$. The missing piece is 60. They need 60 table-spoons of syrup.

This *exact same problem* might also look like this:

$$12 : 2 :: ?:10$$

Those middle four dots are the proportion sign, and this is the same proportion as before. The outsides of the pro-portion, 12 and 10, are called the **extremes**. The insides are called the **means**. If you multiply the extremes by each other, their product will equal the product of the means times each other.

$$12 : 2 :: ?? \; 10$$

So, 120 = 2 × ? again. And again divide both sides by 2 and you find that the missing piece is 60.

   ✎   ✎   ✎   ✎   ✎

"So if we have sixty tablespoons of syrup and ten tablespoons of lemon juice, we have seventy tablespoons altogether? Seventy tablespoons." Jennifer took another sip of the now sweet, tart, delicious lemonade. "Let's go show Sondra and Beauregard what a fine product we've created."

"It's alright, I guess," said Taylor.

When you set up proportions to find a missing piece, you can set them up a variety of ways. If you are saying, for example, that you want a mud recipe that is 2 parts water to 3 parts dirt, and you have 12 cups of dirt, you can set it up two ways. The first way we have already seen. The ratios are placed side by side. All you have to do is make sure both ratios are in the same order, in this case, dirt over water.

$$\frac{3}{2} = \frac{12}{?} \begin{matrix} \leftarrow \text{dirt} \\ \leftarrow \text{water} \end{matrix}$$

The other way is to have the dirt all on one side, and all the water on the other side. Again, order matters. If we put dirt over available dirt, then we must put water over available water.

$$\begin{matrix} \text{dirt} \longrightarrow \\ \text{available dirt} \longrightarrow \end{matrix} \frac{3}{12} = \frac{12}{?} \begin{matrix} \leftarrow \text{water} \\ \leftarrow \text{available water} \end{matrix}$$

Try to cross-multiply both ways. You always get

$$24 = 3 \times ?$$

So the missing piece is 8, because 24 divided by 3 is 8. Any way you slice it, you have the piece you are looking for. As long as you keep on top of the order, you can organize a lot of math any way you want.

"Perfect lemonade," said Jennifer as she kept sipping. They were back in the kitchen after Sondra did a taste test.

"And the boss lady loved it," said Taylor sarcastically.

Taylor and Jennifer did some planning. They decided that their lemonade was so fabulous they should make a huge batch.

"I think we could *easily* sell twenty-eight gallons of the stuff," said Jennifer. "How much syrup will we need then?"

"Don't look at me, I'm just the kitchen help. Sondra's the business manager. She's the big brains around here. I'm a nobody in this organization, a flunky. Let's stand up for our rights. Let's unionize. You threaten to drink all the lemonade unless we get better working conditions. Ha! That'll show 'em."

"Taylor, why don't you just start thinking about how much syrup and sugar we're going to need," said Jennifer.

"Okay, okay," grumbled Taylor. "Fine."

Another thing you can do with ratios and proportions is target how much of a mixture you want to make. For lemonade, you know the ratio is 12 parts syrup to 2 parts lemon juice. Say you wanted to make 28 gallons of lemonade, how much syrup and juice would you need? Well, you know that ratios are set up part to part; here is where the whole comes in. If the lemonade ratio is 12 to 2, what is the whole?

12:2 ratio

$$12 + 2 = 14$$

The whole is 14. Now, you can set up what is called a **ratio box**. A ratio box helps make ratios more explicit. You put in the ratio and the whole, then the amount you want.

Ratio box	Part (Syrup)	Part (Lemon juice)	Whole
Basic ratio	12	2	14
Multiplied by			
Total			28

Now, what did 14 get multiplied by to become 28? (Yet another reason to memorize your times tables.) Fourteen was multiplied by 2 to become 28. Put 2 in the "multiplied by" slot.

Ratio box	Part (Syrup)	Part (Lemon juice)	Whole
Basic ratio	12	2	14
Multiplied by			×2
Total			28

The cool thing is, whatever the whole was multiplied by, the parts were multiplied by too, because the ratio will always stay the same, no matter how many millions of gallons of a mixture you want to make. So, multiply the parts by 2 to see how many you will need.

Ratio box	Part (Syrup)	Part (Lemon juice)	Whole
Basic ratio	12	2	14
Multiplied by	×2	×2	×2
Total	24	4	28

Twenty-four gallons of syrup and 4 gallons of lemon juice. Now here's the kicker, add the 24 and the 4 together—they add up to the 28 gallons of lemonade! Exactly what you wanted. You can check yourself by making sure the parts add up to the whole.

The other way to look at problems like this is to convert the ratio to a real fraction. Since the ratio is 12 to 2, syrup to juice, the total is 14. The fractional part of the lemonade that is juice is $\frac{2}{14}$, or $\frac{1}{7}$ if you reduce it. That is a part over the whole. And the fractional part that is syrup is $\frac{12}{14}$, or $\frac{6}{7}$ if you reduce it. So if you want to know how much juice there is in 28 gallons of lemonade, find $\frac{1}{7}$ of 28.

$$\frac{1}{7} \times 28 = 4$$

What about syrup? Since syrup is $\frac{6}{7}$ of the whole, out of 28 gallons, $\frac{6}{7}$ is syrup.

$$\frac{6}{7} \times 28 = 24$$

You get the same numbers, and you get a whole new appreciation of why multiplying fractions is helpful for a lot of things.

But the ratio box is a terrific thing, and probably the easiest way to look at ratios and proportions. In fact, you can use the ratio box even if you are looking for only part. Say you wanted to make lemonade and only had 6 cups of lemon juice.

Ratio box	Part (Syrup)	Part (Lemon juice)	Whole
Basic ratio	12	2	14
Multiplied by			
Total		6	

Since there were 6 cups of lemon juice, you know you multiplied the 2 by 3 to get the 6. You just multiply everything else by 3.

Ratio box	Part (Syrup)	Part (Lemon juice)	Whole
Basic ratio	12	2	14
Multiplied by	×3	×3	×3
Total	36	6	

Thirty-six cups of syrup to 6 cups of lemon juice.

✍ QUIZ #8 ✍
Proportions and Ratios

1. Simplify the ratio 4:6

2. Find the missing piece in the proportion 2 : 3 :: 8 : ?

3. Find the missing piece in the proportion $\dfrac{4}{5} = \dfrac{12}{?}$

4. Find the missing piece in the proportion $\dfrac{3}{4} = \dfrac{6}{?}$

5. Find the missing piece in the proportion $\dfrac{1}{1} = \dfrac{3}{?}$

6. If Sondra has a box with 4 cassettes and 8 compact discs in it, what is the ratio of compact discs to cassettes in the box? Put the ratio in its most reduced form.

7. Taylor is making cement with only sand and water, and using 3 cups of sand for every 2 cups of water. If he wants to make 15 cups of cement, how much water will he need?

8. Taylor is making glue out of flour and water (this actually works, you can try it yourself). If he uses 1 tablespoon of water for every 3 tablespoons of flour, and he makes 12 tablespoons of glue. How many tablespoons of flour did he use?

9. Taylor and Jennifer own a book collection. The books are fiction and nonfiction. The ratio of fiction to nonfiction is 2:1. If they own 21 books altogether, how many fiction books are in the collection?

10. Jennifer wants to create a powerful love potion. She has heard that you should mix ice cream and hot fudge in a ratio of 3 to 1. If she wants to make 16 gallons of the love potion, how much hot fudge will she need?

✎ ✎ ✎ ✎ ✎

"We're ready!" announced Jennifer as she and Taylor marched into the living room with a pitcher of delicious, icy lemonade. "Let's make some money. We know how much of everything we need."

"Hold on," said Sondra. "We need to set prices and calculate profits and see if we need to set up a separate account for the money we're going to put aside for tax purposes."

"You're making my head hurt," groaned Jennifer. "I need a glass of the sweet stuff, anyone else?"

Everybody wanted a taste of the excellent lemonade, so they each took a glass and sat down to listen to Sondra's plan.

"The situation has changed. We're going to charge one dollar a cup, and we're going to need more ingredients. Let's think big. For every cup of lemonade that costs one dollar, I want us to spend fifty percent of that on ingredients," Sondra said.

Fifty **percent**? You might be thinking, what the heck is a percent anyway? Well, percents are just fractions. You know how decimals are a smaller group of fractions whose denominators are powers of 10? Well, percents are an even smaller group of fractions: percents are fractions with denominators of 100. Remember when we talked about "cent" meaning "one hundred"? Well, per cent means per 100. So fifty percent means fifty for every one hundred parts. Fifty percent, also written as 50%, is actually $\frac{50}{100}$.

All percents can be translated into fractions with denominators of 100, so 50% is equal to $\frac{50}{100}$. You can also reduce the fraction to a smaller fraction. Drop the zeroes from $\frac{50}{100}$

and it becomes $\frac{5}{10}$, then $\frac{5}{10}$ becomes $\frac{1}{2}$. But you must drop the same number of zeros from the top and the bottom. Remember—what's done to the top must be done to the bottom so that the value of the fraction never changes.

How can you translate a percent into a decimal? Drop the percent sign and move the decimal point two spaces to the left.

$$60\% \text{ becomes } 0.60$$

$$2\% \text{ becomes } 0.02$$

Try converting another percent: 35%. Make it into a decimal first. Drop the percent sign and move the decimal point two spaces to the left.

$$35\% = 0.35$$

Now, as a fraction, thirty-five percent is $\frac{35}{100}$. Can you reduce it? Try it by five.

$$\frac{35}{100} \div \frac{5}{5} = \frac{7}{20}$$

You can also convert a fraction into a percent. Multiply the fraction by 1, in the form of a number over itself, to provide a denominator of 100.

Let's try to convert $\frac{2}{25}$ into a percent. What number could you multiply 25 by to get 100? Either guess, or on a separate part of your page divide 100 by 25. You get 4. So, multiply $\frac{2}{25}$ by $\frac{4}{4}$.

$$\frac{2}{25} \times \frac{4}{4} = \frac{8}{100}$$

This is 8%. You can also look at it as a decimal of 0.08, because it is eight hundredths.

To convert a decimal into a percent, just move the decimal point over two to the right and throw in a percent sign. For instance, 0.08 becomes 8, add the percent sign and you are back to 8%.

By the way, when you have 100% of something, how much do you have? The whole darn thing. One hundred percent is equal to 1, or the whole.

✍ QUIZ #9 ✍
Conversion

1. $\dfrac{1}{2}$ Convert to a decimal and a percent.

2. $\dfrac{3}{4}$ Convert to a decimal and a percent.

3. 0.40   Convert to a fraction and a percent.

4. 30%   Convert to a decimal and a fraction.

5. 20%   Convert to a decimal and a fraction.

6. 29%   Convert to a decimal and a fraction.

7. $\dfrac{7}{10}$ Convert to a decimal and a percent.

8. $\dfrac{3}{50}$ Convert to a decimal and a percent.

9. 0.23   Convert to a fraction and a percent.

10. 0.001   Convert to a fraction and a percent.

✎ ✎ ✎ ✎ ✎

"If we sell a cup of lemonade for one dollar, how much money will we keep if fifty percent goes to materials?" Jennifer wondered. "What is fifty percent of a dollar?"

_____

The key to the answer to Jennifer's question is the word "of." The word "of" means "times" in math language, so what Jennifer wants to know is, what is 50% times $1.00?

To answer this, convert the 50% to either a decimal or a fraction, and multiply. 50% × 1 becomes

$$\frac{50}{100} \times 1 = \frac{50}{100} \text{ or } \frac{1}{2}$$

or 0.50—half of a dollar.

That's 50 cents. Why is it 0.50, instead of 50—without a decimal point? Because we did the calculations in terms of dollars, as in "50% of 1," rather than in terms of cents, as in "50% of 100."

✎ ✎ ✎ ✎ ✎

Jennifer sat on the floor and tried to figure out more about the profits. "What if we wanted to use thirty of the fifty cents we spent on ingredients for just sugar? What percent of the ingredients' cost would thirty cents be?" she wondered.

How do you figure this out? Try to determine what she wants to know. The basic question she asked was, 30 is what percent of 50? You can always set-up percent questions like these as ratios.

$$\frac{30}{50} = \frac{?}{100}$$

By writing the problem that way, she says 30 parts of 50 is the same as an unknown number of parts of 100. The whole she is talking about is 50, the part is 30. The whole of a percent is always 100. Now, just cross-multiply to find the missing piece.

$$3,000 = 50 \times ?$$

Divide both sides by 50 to get the missing piece by itself.

$$60 = \text{missing piece}$$

So, 30 is 60% of 50. You could have approximated as well, couldn't you? Since 30 is more than half of 50, you know that 30 will be more than 50%.

There's one more way to look at this kind of proportion. You still set it up as a proportion.

$$\frac{30}{50} = \frac{?}{100}$$

Then, you look across the equals sign. The 50 was multiplied by something to become 100, and the top half of the fraction was multiplied by the same number. So, what was 50 multiplied by to become 100? Fifty gets multiplied by 2, so the top half gets multiplied by 2 as well, to become 60. You're doing the same problem in a slightly different way.

THINK ABOUT THIS

The rules for multiples of 10% are cool and easy. One hundred percent of something is the whole thing. To find 10%, you just move the decimal point one space over to the left. For 1%, you move the decimal point two spaces to the left. How about for 0.1%? What do you think? You move the decimal point three spaces over to the left. Pretty cool, huh?

100% of 2,356 = 2,356

10% of 2,356 = 235.6

1% of 2,356 = 23.56

0.1% of 2,356 = 2.356

And so on.

✐ ✐ ✐ ✐ ✐

"Okay you guys, I need to figure out something and I want you out of the way while I think," said Sondra.

"But we're involved in this too!" Jennifer protested.

"Well, that's true, but since I'm in charge," Sondra said, "You just have to trust me that this is important."

"Strike! Strike! Strike!" Taylor yelled, pumping his fist in the air. "No more cutbacks . . . no more bosses . . . I'm union and proud of it! Jennifer, drink all the lemonade!" Jennifer put Taylor in a head lock and dragged him back into the kitchen.

By herself in the living room, Sondra did some calculations. She measured how much lemonade they had; only two glasses left! Then she asked Beauregard how much the ingredients would have cost them.

"Gracious, all those lemons and the sugar would have cost two dollars and forty cents!"

And there were only two glasses of lemonade to sell. At one dollar a glass, that would only bring in two dollars. They would take a forty cent loss!

"How am I going to explain this?" she thought to herself. "And what percent loss is that anyway?"

To determine the percent loss, first find the loss. In this case, there is a 40 cent loss. Then, you want to know, "Forty cents is what percent of 200 cents?" (Better known as two dollars but it will be easier to keep everything in the same terms.) Set up a proportion.

$$\frac{40}{200} = \frac{?}{100}$$

You can cross-multiply again.

$4{,}000 = 200 \times ?$

$4{,}000 = 200 \times 20$

Losing 40 cents from 2 dollars is a 20% loss.

YOU CAN ALSO THINK ABOUT THIS

Say you are looking at a multiple of 10%. Someone wants to know what 30% of 200 is, for instance. One quick way to do it is to find 10% of 200. Just move that decimal point over one to the left; 10% of 200 is 20.

Then, since you want 30% and not 10%, just multiply that 10% by 3.

$20 \times 3 = 60$

Since 10% times 3 is 30%, 20 times 3 is 30% of 200. Or, 60 is 30% of 200. There are many different ways to do any math problem, the more ways you can think of, the more comfortable with math you will be.

✍ QUIZ #10 ✍
Percentages

1. $10\% \times 50 =$

2. $25\% \times 16 =$

3. $3\% \times 300 =$

4. $\dfrac{20}{50} = \dfrac{?}{100}$

5. $\dfrac{2}{20} = \dfrac{?}{100}$

6. If Sondra has 10 carrots, and she gives 90% of them to her sister, how many carrots does she have left?

7. Taylor receives 32% of $1000 as a prize in a raffle. How much money does he win?

8. Taylor offers 100% of nothing to his little brother as payment for mowing the lawn. Is it a good deal for Taylor's little brother, and how much will he get?

9. Taylor and Jennifer have 3 out of 30 possible baseball cards. What percent of the baseball cards do they have?

10. The owner of a famous collection of 200 bats loses 1 bat to Jennifer. Her bat represents what percentage loss to the collection?

⬍ ⬍ ⬍ ⬍ ⬍

"Well, what's the story?" Jennifer asked. She'd tied Taylor to a chair with a kitchen apron and stuffed a towel in his mouth to keep him quiet. "How rich are we? Can we buy a Jeep? Or a small Caribbean island?"

"Not exactly," said Sondra. "We seem to have drunk most of the profits, you might say."

"Oh no!" said Jennifer, suddenly feeling guilty. "Is there any hope of saving it?"

"Nope," admitted Sondra. They sat down on the other chairs around the kitchen table to consider the situation.

"Mmmmpf—mmmpff grrggg," Taylor said in a constricted kind of way.

"For once I agree with Taylor," Jennifer commented.

"Grrgmpff mnkrpff mmmpff hhrghthpf!"

"Heavens," said Beauregard. "I wouldn't untie him yet."

✍ QUIZ #11 ✎
Review

1. Rewrite 20% as a fraction and a decimal.

2. $\dfrac{2}{3} = \dfrac{8}{?}$

3. 1 : 3 :: 2 : ?

4. Rewrite $\dfrac{1}{4}$ as a decimal and a percentage.

5. Rewrite $\dfrac{3}{20}$ as a decimal and a percentage.

6. Jennifer needs to buy ink for a special invisible-writing mixture. How many cups of ink are there in a 25 cups of a mixture that has water to ink in a ratio of 2 to 3? What percentage of the mixture is ink?

7. Taylor has to give 14% of his collection of 200 marbles to his little brother (parental punishment after the lawn mower incident). How many marbles does he have to give away? Don't forget to approximate first.

8. If Jennifer makes fake blood using 3 drops of red food coloring for every 1 drop of yellow food coloring (to make it look brown when it dries), how many pints of red food coloring will she need to make 16 pints of fake blood? What percentage of the mixture is yellow food coloring?

9. Jennifer makes 10 gallons of salt water, that is 50% salt, and 50% water. What is the ratio of salt to water in the mixture?

10. Jennifer bought a set of trucks and cars in a ratio of 1 to 5. If there are 15 cars, how many trucks are there in the set?

Jennifer, Taylor, Sondra, and Beauregard stood outside the small tiger-striped house. "Big-head" Jones whizzed past on a bicycle pulling Lucy Skupps on Rollerblades. She was screaming "Faster! Faster!" Poor Big-head, hunched over the handlebars with a grimace of concentration and pain, looked as if he was already pedaling as fast as he could. The sweat poured off his oversize forehead. The kids watched the crazy-looking pair disappear down the block.

"Well, what are other ways to make money? There's selling and trading, but there are skills too, right? Maybe we could win some test of skill," Sondra suggested.

Two old dudes jogged by on rickety legs in shiny red matching shorts.

"I've got it!" Jennifer said, "We'll go over to the high school field where the older kids hang out, and we'll challenge them to races and bet money! They'll never expect me to win."

"Skeezer? Skeezer?" gasped Taylor. "You're going to challenge Skeezer and his pals to a race? This I've got to see."

"I'm the fastest kid around. It's a sure thing. And Skeezer's such a jerk he'll take the bet. I know it. With the money I win I'll buy us all tickets *and* popcorn *and* soda *and* candy. Anyway we can't lose, *right*?"

"It's true," Sondra said. "What a great idea! Why didn't we think of it before? Let's go."

Beauregard looked suspicious of the whole deal. "I don't know about this Skeezer. He's a pretty nasty character as I recall."

"Don't worry about a thing," Sondra and Jennifer said at once.

"Well all right, and my heavens, Jennifer is a fast runner. But I don't like it. You kids go on ahead. I'll follow at a polite distance."

Chapter 6
Probability and Averages

The field at the high school was brown and dried out from the heat. A ragged pair of teenagers stood in the shade against the brick wall. They both looked sour, unpleasant, and bored. Sondra, Taylor, and Jennifer walked straight over and proposed the race.

"We'll make a bet with you," said Sondra. "We'll bet that Jennifer here can beat either of you in the 100-yard dash. If she wins, you guys give us twenty-seven dollars, if she loses . . ."

"Yeah, and what if she loses? What then?" sneered Skeezer, a tall, skinny teenager.

Skeezer. Everyone called him that because he had a weird way of breathing through his nose so that it whistled with a *skeezing* sound. Rumor had it that when Skeezer was a child he'd been named Quincy by his parents, but that was long ago and no one really believed it. He had an awful skin condition that made his face raw, red, and flaking all the time. Skeezer wore faded blue jeans dark with grease, shabby high-top sneakers, and a black leather motorcycle jacket. Because of the sweltering heat his jacket was unzipped. But he never took it off. *Never.* Skeezer had a bad reputation for a number of things, most of them horrible and weird, but he was also known as a fast runner.

"What do we get if she loses?" Skeezer asked again, leering. "You can be sure she's going to lose."

"Nothing that happens in the future is definite," said Jennifer.

Fred, Skeezer's best friend, stood and flapped his arms like an uncoordinated priest. "Strange sausage! Evil eye! Batwing psycho-freaks. I predict a harsh future for all."

No one but Skeezer ever understood much of what Fred was talking about, which was a good thing.

"These guys are really warped," said Taylor. "This was a bad idea. I knew it was a bad idea. Let's go figure out another plan."

"No way," Jennifer said quietly. "I know I can out-race this creep. I know it."

Skeezer overheard her. "No chance. Not one chance in a million, little girl."

"But Skeez-man," Fred said, glaze-eyed, "what if Dr. Mephisto reached down with his glowing iron fist and smashed you into the dirt? What if the earth itself opened and dragged you down to its nether depths, never to be seen again, in this life or *any other*?"

"Shut up, Fred," Skeezer said without even looking at him.

"See, even your friends know it," Sondra said. "Victory is never assured. It's a matter of probability, and you've got the odds figured wrong."

Probability is the mathematical way people talk about the likelihood that something will happen. It is usually expressed in fraction form and is used to figure the chances of random events occurring. In other words, events with outcomes we have no real control over, like flipping a coin. One chance in a million would look like this: $\dfrac{1}{1,000,000}$. The top part indicates how many successful possibilities there are, and the bottom part indicates the number of total possibilities. This particular probability also implies that the other side—that Skeezer will win the race, in this case—is very likely to happen. They would say he has a $\dfrac{999,999}{1,000,000}$ chance of winning the race.

The bigger the fraction, the more likely a successful outcome is. The smaller the fraction, the less likely the successful outcome is. The maximum probability is 1. A sure thing has a probability of 1. Out of a million chances, it will happen every time. Say you flipped a 2-headed coin 1 million times. Every time the coin will land on heads, therefore the probability of getting heads is 1. $\dfrac{1,000,000}{1,000,000} = 1$. Something that has already happened has a probability of 1. People don't often talk about the probability of things that have already happened, though.

Another way something can be a sure thing is the opposite, if you are sure that something *won't* happen. The probability of getting tails when you are flipping a 2-headed coin is 0. Out of 1 million flips, none are tails, so $\dfrac{0}{1,000,000} = 0$.

✑ ✑ ✑ ✑ ✑

"Here's my proposal," Skeezer said craftily. "Let's run three races and the best out of three wins."

"I don't know; I don't trust this guy," Taylor murmured to Sondra. "Something about this doesn't seem right."

"Come on, *babies*," teased Skeezer. "If your runner is so great, what's the problem?"

"All right, we'll do it," said Jennifer. "I accept the challenge. Everyone knows girls are better endurance runners than boys, anyway." She looked at the others. "If we win we get twenty-seven dollars."

"And if you lose," Skeezer said. "You have to be our slaves for the rest of the day!"

Taylor turned ash gray. Sondra was too stunned to speak and just shook her head back and forth like it wasn't possible. Jennifer stuck out her arm and shook Skeezer's raw, flaky, red hand before any of the others could say a word.

"No problem," said Jennifer. "This guy's a pushover."

"Three races of one hundred each then," said Skeezer.

"This guy Skeezer is a total low-life," said Sondra. "I can feel it in my bones. He's up to something. What should we do?"

"Don't worry about a thing," Jennifer whispered. "I'm going to whip him, fair and square."

"To make the whole race scientific, because we don't have videotapes to check the finish or anything, why don't we just time the three races and then take the average? What could be more fair than that?" said Skeezer. "You kids don't think I would *cheat* or anything? You look kinda nervous."

"It sounds okay to me," Jennifer said.

"And just to prove what a nice guy I am, I'm going to let you go first," said Skeezer.

"I don't need any special favors."

"No, please," said Skeezer. "It would be my pleasure."

"Well, here goes," said Jennifer. She stood at the starting line, in the heat, and put her fingertips to the ground in a perfect four-point sprinter's crouch.

"Alright, three timed races of one hundred each. Agreed?" Skeezer said.

"Yes, yes, we agreed already, let's do it!" said Jennifer.

"On your mark. Get set." Taylor held a stopwatch high in the air. He brought his arm down, yelling, "Go!"

Jennifer flew down the track and when she hit the 100-yard mark, Taylor clicked his stopwatch. "Thirteen seconds!" he shouted.

Then Skeezer ran. His clumsy movements gave the impression that he didn't have enough bones in his body to run or that his joints were somehow too loose, but his long legs took big bites out of the track and his time was a respectable fifteen seconds. Even so, Jennifer already had a 2-second edge. Sondra cheered. Taylor allowed himself a slight smile. The second race began. Jennifer slipped and fell just as she started, but she got up again quickly and sprinted off.

"Seventeen seconds," Taylor said glumly.

Fortunately, Skeezer had his own problems. He started off blazing, and everyone was sure he'd have the best time of the afternoon, but only a few yards from the finish he pulled up short in a fit of coughing, and only after several seconds had passed did he manage to stagger across the finish line.

"Nineteen seconds for Skeezer," said Taylor.

Sondra cheered. Taylor didn't even smile though. He noticed that Skeezer didn't look the slightest bit concerned. Because the times were going to be averaged, Skeezer would have to win the last race by several seconds if he was to have any hope of winning the contest, but he didn't even look worried.

Taylor worried. What were their averages so far?

An **average** is a number expressing the norm of a group of numbers. It is also called the **arithmetic mean**. To find the average of a group of numbers, add all the numbers in the group, then divide by how many numbers are in the group.

For example, Jennifer's times were 13 seconds and 17 seconds. So first, add all the numbers in the group.

$$13 + 17 = 30$$

Then, divide by how many numbers are in the group. How many numbers are in the group? 2.

$$30 \div 2 = 15$$

Jennifer's average time is 15 seconds.

Try again with Skeezer's average. The first race he ran was 15 seconds, the second race was 19 seconds. First, find the total of the numbers in the group.

$$15 + 19 = 34$$

Then, divide that total by how many numbers are in the group, again, in this case, 2.

$$34 \div 2 = 17$$

Skeezer's average time is 17 seconds.

✎ ✎ ✎ ✎ ✎

Jennifer had also noticed that Skeezer seemed a little too calm. He's been holding back, she thought. He's going to run like the wind this last race, I know it. I've got to do better.

She got down in her stance and when Taylor yelled "Go!" she almost flew down the track. Her feet barely touched the ground, she ran like a greyhound, she ran so fast the other kids fell silent and the only sound anyone could hear was the pounding of her feet on the dirt track. "*Nine* seconds!" Taylor yelled in excitement. "Wait a minute, I think that's the world's record!"

Sondra cheered, "Jennifer! Jennifer! She's our girl! She's the fastest in the world!" She turned to Skeezer. "Okay, Skeeza-reeno, your turn, if you even want to bother, or you can just pay up now and spare yourself the embarrassing trouble of running."

"Gimme the stopwatch, shorty," Skeezer said to Taylor. "I'll time myself. I'm tired of getting cheated by you losers. World record? Gimme a break. Now hand over that watch, moon-face."

Skeezer loomed over Taylor and sneered. Taylor gave him the watch. Skeezer took his position, yelled "Go!" to himself, walked just two short, slow steps, and clicked the watch. "Two seconds!" Skeezer said triumphantly. "Hey slaves, I'm the winner, as usual."

"But you didn't finish the race," said Taylor. "You haven't run the whole way."

"I just said it was a race of one hundred," Skeezer explained. "I never said one hundred *yards*; you dweeb-brains just assumed that."

Fred erupted in howls of delight. "Another victory for Evil and Vicious Mayhem!"

"Oh no!" cried Taylor. "He's right! He did say a race of one hundred, and I thought it sounded strange but I didn't know why."

Jennifer stood by huffing and puffing and sweating from having run so fast.

Skeezer put his hands on his skinny hips. "I just ran one hundred centimeters. Now you guys have to be our slaves. Just compare the average times!"

What are their average times now? You find an average by adding the numbers in the group then dividing by how many numbers are in the group, right? So Jennifer's times need to be added.

$$13 + 17 + 9 = 39$$

Now you divide by how many numbers are in the group. There are 3 this time.

$$39 \div 3 = 13$$

Jennifer's average time is 13 seconds.

Skeezer's average time can be figured out the same way. Have you figured it out yet?

$$15 + 19 + 2 = 36$$

Then divide by 3, because that's how many numbers there are in the group.

$$36 \div 3 = 12$$

Skeezer's average time is 12 seconds, the creep.

✎ ✎ ✎ ✎ ✎

"This is totally unfair and somebody is going to pay," said Sondra.

"Yeah, *you*," Skeezer said, leaning down into Sondra's face so close that she could smell his breath. It stank like a grotty old foot.

"Gracious me," said Beauregard, who'd watched the whole incident from a polite distance, "but you agreed to take the average, didn't you?"

"Hey, beat it, pussycat. Shouldn't you be scratching a post somewhere? You just heard us calculate the average and your little pals lost, so scram!"

"Oh my, yes, but that was the arithmetic *mean*, and I don't recall you all agreeing on *that*. There are other kinds of averages you know, take the *median* for instance."

What is a **median**? Well, in a set of numbers ordered from smallest to largest, the median is the middle number. Jennifer's set of times, arranged in order, is this: 9, 13, 17. Jennifer's median time is 13 seconds, because 13 is the number in the middle. Skeezer's set of times, arranged in order, is this: 2, 15, 19. The middle number is 15, so Skeezer's median time is 15 seconds.

What if there is an even number of samples in a group? For instance, if someone runs 4 races? Well then, find the 2 middle numbers, and find their average (arithmetic mean).

APPROXIMATE THIS

What do think is the fastest time ever to run the 100-yard dash?

✎ ✎ ✎ ✎ ✎

"Listen up, fur-face," glared Skeezer. "Forget that median thing. When people say average everybody knows they're talking about the arithmetic mean—so that's the rule."

"But people always mean one hundred *yards* too," said Beauregard. "Oh yes, and there's another kind of average too, the *mode*."

"How about if we measure the mode?" said Taylor.

What is a **mode**? A mode is the number that appears most frequently in a group of numbers. Since no number appears more than once in the times that Jennifer and Skeezer ran, because they took a different amount of time to run each race, their sets of times have no modes. But what is the mode of this set of numbers?

7, 3, 6, 5, 6, 19

The mode of that set of numbers is 6, because 6 appears twice, while all the other numbers appear only once.

How about this next set of numbers?

$$4, 8, 9, 8, 4, 5, 7, 4, 9$$

The mode of that set is 4, because it appears three times, as opposed to 8 and 9, which only appear twice each.

What about this set?

$$1, 5, 3, 1, 5, 7$$

This is what is called a **bimodal** sample, because two numbers appear more than once but the same number of times as each other. The two modes of this sample are 1 and 5. Bimodal means there are two modes, but it won't happen a whole lot.

✍ QUIZ #12 ✍
Average, Median, Mode

1. What is the average of 2, 3, and 4?

2. What is the average of 3 and 7?

3. What is the average of 1, 3, 6, 3, and 7?

4. What is the median of the group of numbers in question 3?

5. Now, what is the mode of the group of numbers in question 3?

6. On Monday Sondra biked 3 miles, on Tuesday she biked 6 miles, and on Wednesday she biked 15 miles. What was the average number of miles that Sondra biked per day over those 3 days?

7. Sondra, who (in case you didn't notice) was on some kind of physical fitness kick, did 14 push-ups on Thursday, 12 push-ups on Friday, and 10 push-ups on Saturday. Sondra did how many push-ups on average per day over Thursday, Friday, and Saturday? Also, just to approximate, would her average increase or decrease if you just took the average of Thursday and Saturday?

8. Taylor is checking out prices on hats, because the sun has been getting to him just a little too much recently. At the hat store, he looks at six hats. One of them is 2 dollars, two of them are 3 dollars each, two of them are 4 dollars each, and one of them is 8 dollars. What is the average price of the hats Taylor looks at?

9. Taylor and Jennifer are counting how many people on average live in the seven houses on their block. Three of the houses hold 8 people each, and the other four houses hold 1 person each. How many people live in the average house on their block?

10. Jennifer is measuring how high she can jump. She jumps five times and these are the heights of her jumps: 20 inches, 29 inches, 26 inches, 20 inches, and 25 inches. What is the average height of her jumps? What is the mode? What is the median?

✎ ✎ ✎ ✎ ✎

Skeezer slid his hands into his back pockets, leaned back, and breathed out—*skeeeeeeeeze*—through his nose. "Alright, you got me, it's a tie. I won the mean average and you won the median average. Fair's fair, right? But we do have to settle this bet, so let's get it settled. You decided what the first contest would be; I'll decide the next one. Fair's fair, after all. Okay. We'll wrestle. Me against one of you squirts here." He was looking right at Taylor when he said it.

"Wrestle you?" gulped Taylor. "You'd *kill* me." Taylor turned to his friends, "He'd kill me." They all nodded, even Beauregard.

"I wouldn't *kill* you squirt, I'd certainly hurt you badly, maybe leave you maimed for life, but kill? Nah, I probably wouldn't do that."

"This is so typical. Jennifer has the rotten idea to race Mr. Skeezer here, Sondra agrees to it, they both get tricked, and the one person who thought this was all completely retarded, *me*, I have to wrestle Skeezer. No way. I won't do it."

"Well that settles that," Skeezer said, "Okay, slaves, my first command is . . ."

"Wait a minute, wait a minute, I'll wrestle you," Jennifer said. "Taylor's not the only one who can wrestle."

"I'm not going to wrestle a girl," Skeezer said.

"Why not? Oh, you make me sick, you're nothing but a mmmpphf"—Jennifer tried to say something, but Taylor clamped his hand over her mouth and whispered, "Jennifer, shhhh, you're only making things worse!"

"Heavens, I've got the answer!" Beauregard said as pleasantly as always. "Why, I'd be honored to wrestle this charming gentleman."

For some reason, this time when Beauregard smiled the kids suddenly noticed how long and sharp his teeth were, and when he extended his arm to shake Skeezer's hand the claws on Beauregard's paw glinted in the sun.

Skeezer noticed too, "Aw, now, now, now, wait a gosh darn minute, I just had an another idea, yeah, sure a great idea, I mean I wouldn't want to hurt an animal or anything, heck. I think we ought to just flip a coin. How does that sound?"

"You're sure you wouldn't rather wrestle?" Beauregard asked sweetly.

"Oh, I'd love to wrestle, but I'd hate for you to get hurt, you understand."

"Likewise," said Beauregard.

The kids agreed. A coin toss had to be fair.

Jennifer flipped the coin high into the air. At the last moment Skeezer called it: tails. The coin smacked into the dirt at their feet. Heads.

"Okay, that's one for me," Skeezer said triumphantly. "The tails side is the one against the dirt *just like I called.*"

"Oh my God! I can't stand it! You are such a cheater! You cheat so bad I'm going crazy." Taylor pounded his fist against his thigh.

"A cheater? What are you talking about, Squirty? Oh, wait a minute, do you mean to tell me you call coins by the side that *shows*? By the face-up side instead of the side it lands on? Huh . . . okay, let's do it your way, I guess we'd better do it over. See what a fair guy I am?"

The truth is Skeezer figured he had an advantage even in the do over. The coin had come up heads the first time; so he thought that now the more probable result would be tails, which would even things out. But Skeezer, as you might have guessed, doesn't understand probability. Skeezer thinks that because the coin flipped to heads first, it is more likely to flip to tails next. This isn't true. Two separate flips are what is known as **independent events**. That means the first flip and the second flip have nothing to do with each other; they don't affect each other's outcome at all. After all, a coin has no memory of past events. It will flip randomly no matter what. Since there are two possible outcomes, and an equal chance of getting either, the probability of getting heads is $\frac{1}{2}$, and of getting tails is $\frac{1}{2}$. No matter how many flips you do, each coin toss has the same probability of going heads or tails, provided you have a fair coin.

There are several ways to find the probability of several unrelated events. Let's say you were going to flip a coin three times, and you wanted to know the probability that you would get all heads. One way to find out is to list them. How many possible outcomes are there?

HHH, HHT, HTH, HTT, TTT, TTH, THT, THH

There are eight possible outcomes. What is the probability that you will get all heads? There is only one way out of eight possible ways that this can happen, so the probability is $\frac{1}{8}$.

The way to do this quickly is to multiply the probabilities. That means, find the probability of getting heads the first toss: $\frac{1}{2}$. Then the probability of getting heads on the second toss is $\frac{1}{2}$, and the same for the third toss. So the 3 probabilities are $\frac{1}{2}$, $\frac{1}{2}$, and $\frac{1}{2}$. To find the probabilities of getting all 3 heads, just multiply these.

$$\frac{1}{2} \times \frac{1}{2} \times \frac{1}{2} = \frac{1}{8}$$

This works for any independent events. If you have 2 separate bags, each with 1 red marble and 1 blue marble, and you choose 1 marble from each bag, what is the probability both chosen marbles will be blue? Well, the probability that the marble chosen will be blue is $\frac{1}{2}$ in both cases, so the probability that both will be blue is $\frac{1}{2} \times \frac{1}{2}$, or $\frac{1}{4}$.

✍ QUIZ #13 ✍
Probability

1. If you have a bag with 5 Lifesavers in it, 2 red, 2 orange, and 1 green, what is the probability that if you just stick your hand in and choose randomly, the Lifesaver you choose will be green?

2. In that same bag with the same 5 Lifesavers in it, what is the probability that you will choose a red Lifesaver?

3. Same old bag of 5, but now you are finding the probability that you will choose a white Lifesaver.

4. You now have two of those bags of Lifesavers, and you are choosing 1 from the first bag, then 1 from the second bag. What is the probability that both Lifesavers will be green?

5. Same situation as question 4, but what is the probability that both Lifesavers will be orange?

✎ ✎ ✎ ✎ ✎

"You know something?" said Beauregard. "I don't think we need to toss the coin again."

"What?" everyone asked.

"Skeezer, you didn't start out with fair intentions, and you've proved to me that you don't ever have them. Jennifer, Taylor, Sondra, you didn't listen carefully enough, and you agreed to the terms. If you start acting dishonestly now, you'll end up just like these two gentlemen in a few years."

"I don't think I'll ever end up like those jerks," Jennifer said loud enough for Skeezer and his pal to hear as she and the kids walked away. "I'll never race that slow."

By the way, can you tell how fast Jennifer ran? Just think back to proportions for a minute. If Jennifer went 100 yards in 10 seconds, how fast was she going per second?

Well, set up a proportion:

$$\frac{100}{10} = \frac{?}{1}$$

Cross-multiply.

$$100 = 10 \times ?$$

And divide.

$$100 = 10 \times 10 \text{ so } ? = 10$$

Jennifer ran 10 yards per second. Remember her actual time in the last race against Skeezer? She went 100 yards in 9 seconds, which is even faster, slightly more than 11 yards a second. Pretty impressive.

Most rates are really just proportions. Since rates are usually given as miles per hour or yards per second, you can remember back to percents, where you learned that "per" means divide. So, just divide whenever it says per, and that is your rate. But be careful not to forget the lesson Jennifer and the others just learned about terms of measurement. If you are changing units of measurement, say seconds to minutes, or minutes to hours, just set up as a proportion instead of dividing. A proportion will always work if you set it up correctly.

✎ ✎ ✎ ✎ ✎

Jennifer, Taylor, Sondra, and Beauregard walked arm in arm back toward their neighborhood.

"Oh well," said Taylor, "one more busted-up plan. Just like always, nothing ever works. I was right the whole time. We should have stayed under the tree all day and complained. We'd have gotten just as much accomplished with a lot less work."

"I'm actually starting to agree with Taylor," Jennifer said.

"Well, at least we've had some fun," Sondra protested.

"Oh yeah, huge fun, incredible," Taylor said sarcastically. "The only tough part is figuring out which was more fun, almost getting pounded by Skeezer or cleaning up the mess Jennifer made. Let's have *more* fun. Maybe we could stick our faces in a wasps' nest? Or how about we scrape our teeth against a chalkboard? I've got it. Let's change into really, really tight, uncomfortable clothing, put on brand new shoes that are two sizes too small with sand up near the toe, then stand perfectly still for nine hours on one foot. Doesn't that sound great? Not as great as almost getting creamed by Skeezer, of course, but pretty close, huh?"

"Come on, Taylor. It wasn't that bad," Sondra said. "And anyway, what should we do now? Wait a sec. Okay, Mr. Negative . . . let's decide what we *won't* do.

"No bicycling. I *despise* bicycling," Taylor said.

"All right, no complaining. I think complaining stinks," Jennifer glared at him.

"Fine," said Taylor. "No eating, no food of *any kind.*"

"Hold on a second, Beauregard and I get choices too," Sondra said. "I say no arguing."

"Excellent," Beauregard said. "That gets my vote too, no disagreeing."

"Okay," said Sondra. "Now, let's pick two things from our list of things-not-to-do. We'll vote. Everyone gets two votes, one for the thing they most do not want to do, and one for the thing they second-most do not want to do."

Everyone has five choices to pick from: Arguing, Bicycling, Complaining, Disagreeing, and Eating. We'll call them A, B, C, D, and E. How many possible choices are there? To figure that out you first have to realize that the order matters because the first choice is for the worst thing to do, and the second choice is for the next worst thing to do. (Another way to think of this is that *position* matters.) For example, if you picked BA, that would be different from picking AB. When you are choosing possible arrangements from a group, or figuring out how many possible arrangements there are, those arrangements are called **permutations.**

One way to figure out permutations is to simply work your way through them slowly. List all possibilities if you choose A first.

AB, AC, AD, AE. Four possibilities.

Now try to list all the possible combinations to combine with B.

BA, BC, BD, BE.

Four again. Remember: BA isn't the same as AB. We said order mattered.

Now, how many combinations can you make with the next letter, C?

CA, CB, CD, CE.

And D?

DA, DB, DC, DE.

Then all that is left is E and, as you probably predicted, there are four possibilities with E as well. EA, EB, EC, ED. Now, add all the possibilities together.

$$4 + 4 + 4 + 4 + 4 = 20$$

There are twenty different possibilities to choose from.

There is another way to determine permutations, but if you ever get confused, go back to just listing them. To figure them quickly, ask yourself how many possibilities are there for the first spot? In this case, how many activities could be the first one? 5. Then, once you have written down that, how many possibilities are there for the second spot? Since you can't do the same activity twice, there are only 4 possibilities. And that's it, multiply your two possibilities:

$$5 \times 4 = 20$$

That's how many permutations there are. Pretty slick, wouldn't you say?

How about if you weren't choosing 2? How about if you were seeing how many possible arrangements there were for all 5? You do it the same way. How many possibilities for the first space? 5. The second? 4. The third? 3. The fourth space? 2. The fifth space? Only 1 left. Now multiply.

$$5 \times 4 \times 3 \times 2 \times 1 = 120$$

There are 120 possible arrangements of the 5 activities.

There is another way to choose that is a little different: without regard to order. How about choosing from a whole roster of activities for a day?

Let's see if we can make a perfect day. In the morning you can do one of three things: take a stroll in a meadow full of spring flowers; sail in a glorious, sparkling blue bay; or eat a huge breakfast snuggled up in bed.

In the afternoon you can: go for a leisurely swim in a sparkling blue lake; go to the zoo to see the new anteater from Africa; or go rollerskating on the new high-speed circuit in the park.

In the evening you can: play miniature golf on your new course; waltz under the stars with your favorite movie star; or go to a new carnival with the biggest freak show on the planet.

How many different combinations are there? **Combinations**. Pretty logical name, wouldn't you say? Well, let's rename our choices to make them easier to use. Call the morning activities A, B, and C; the afternoon D, E, and F; and the evening G, H, and I.

As before, start with the first, A. Now how many can you have with A?

ADG, ADH, ADI, AEG, AEH, AEI, AFG, AFH, AFI.

There are 9 possible combinations with A.

How many with B? Think about it, probably the same number, but try it to see.

BDG, BDH, BDI, BEG, BEH, BEI, BFG, BFH, BFI.

Nine again!

So how many combinations with C? You know it must be 9. Altogether, the 3 groups of 9 add up to 27.

There is a faster way to do this, of course. Ask yourself how many possibilities there are in the morning? 3. In the afternoon? 3. In the evening? 3. To find out how many in total, multiply the possibilities.

$$3 \times 3 \times 3 = 27$$

✍ QUIZ #14 ✍
Permutations and Combinations

1. Taylor has 3 flowers—a rose, a violet, and a peony. If he lines them up in a row on the counter, how many arrangements can he make?

2. Sondra is arranging prizes she won at the fair on the wall of her bedroom. She won 4 prizes (she knocked down 20 toy cats with a baseball), and she is putting only 2 on the wall of her room, because she is saving the other 2 for the kitchen. How many possible arrangements of 2 prizes on her wall are there?

3. Taylor is building a spaceship. If there are 3 possible engines, 2 possible hull designs, and 2 possible interior designs, and he has to choose one of each to make a total spaceship plan, how many possible total spaceship plans are there?

4. Jennifer and Taylor are packing their ration box for a camping trip. There are 2 kinds of fruit, 3 kinds of bread, and 2 kinds of cheese to choose from, and they must only choose 1 of each. How many possible menus are there for the ration box?

5. Sondra is performing in a gymnastics competition, and she has to choose 3 moves from a group of 10 possible moves to arrange her opening sequence. None of the moves can be repeated. How many opening sequences are possible if she is choosing only from this group?

✍ QUIZ #15 ✍
Review

1. In a bag with only 2 marbles, red and black, what is the probability that Rose will choose a green marble?

2. If Rose must choose 1 marble at random from a bag with 20 marbles in it (5 red, 3 blue, 10 green, and 2 yellow) what is the probability that the marble she chooses will be blue?

3. Lionel has 2 turtles, Grace and Mike. If the 2 turtles run 10 races of the same distance, and Mike completes a total of 10 races in 5 minutes, and Grace completes a total of 10 races in 7 minutes, which turtle has a faster average time per race?

4. If Lionel has a box with 10 balls in it, 5 blue and 5 red, and he chooses 1 ball at random, what is the probability that the ball he chooses will be red?

5. If Sondra chooses a ball from a box with 10 blue balls, what is the probability that the ball she chooses will be blue?

6. Two years ago Sondra was 50 inches tall, last year Sondra was 53 inches tall, and this year Sondra is 56 inches tall. What is Sondra's average height over the past three years?

7. Taylor has three snorkeling masks. One of the masks weighs 16 ounces, the second weighs 18 ounces, and the third weighs 20 ounces. What is the average weight of the three masks?

8. Taylor is making a tape for a friend, and he is trying to decide which 3 songs to put first, and in what order, out of 7 songs. How many possible arrangements are there for the first 3 songs?

9. Jennifer swam 1 mile 5 times last week, when she was visiting her cousin at the ocean. Her times for each mile were, 20 minutes, 23 minutes, 20 minutes, 24 minutes, and 18 minutes the morning she tried coffee for the first time. What was her average time per mile, the mode, and the median of her times?

10. Jennifer has a box with 1 blue marble, 1 green marble, and 1 red marble in it. (A lot of these strange boxes of marbles floating around, don't you think?) If she chooses a marble at random and, then replaces it 4 times in a row, what is the probability that she will choose a blue marble all 4 times?

Chapter 7
Graphs and Charts

Things didn't work out the way they thought things would. Beauregard was curled up in his favorite nook high in the oak tree. Taylor lay nestled among the roots daydreaming about all the horrible things that would undoubtedly happen to him someday. Jennifer zoomed around and around the tree on her bicycle

"This is ridiculous!" Sondra shouted. "We're right back where we started. I can't stand it. Everyone is doing exactly what we just agreed we wouldn't do."

"Including you! You're arguing," Taylor said. "Of course we're right back where we started. Nothing has worked, nothing has turned out right. Nothing ever turns out right. Everything *stinks*. I was a fool to even hope. Now that I've lost all hope I feel much better though."

"But you're wrong, Taylor. Things have happened, and things have changed. Look, I'll show you." Sondra drew on the pavement with a piece of chalk. When she was through, she called Taylor and Jennifer over. "Now I've drawn a graph here charting happiness over the day. I've decided to measure happiness in smiles per minute. I think we can all agree that I am the most willing to smile, generally?

"See, I've charted the day starting at 9 a.m., and my average smiles per minute every hour from then till now. It's three o'clock now."

"You keep track of your smiles per minute?" Jennifer gaped. "And I thought Taylor was a wacko."

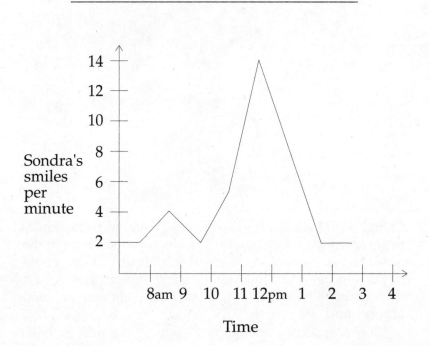

A **line graph** uses lines to show information. The vertical line, where the number of smiles per minute is listed on this graph, is sometimes called the **Y axis**, and the horizontal line, where the time of day is listed on this graph, is sometimes called the **X axis**. To read a line graph, start at one of the **axes** (that's plural for axis and pronounced acks-eez). Say you wanted to know how many times Sondra smiled at 2 p.m. Look at the 2 p.m. spot on the time axis and follow it up till you see the graphed line. Then, look to the left to see how many smiles per minute correspond with the place graphed. Sondra smiled 2 times, on average, at 2 p.m.

✎ ✎ ✎ ✎ ✎

"What I'm trying to show is that things have been going up and down all day. We weren't very happy when the day started. Then we were happy eating lunch at Beauregard's, unhappy cleaning up, happy when Jennifer faked us out, unhappy when we realized the air conditioning had shut down. Then there's the whole lemonade episode, and *here*"—Sondra pointed to the end of the chart, indicating a deep dip in the happiness line at 2:00 p.m.— "is where we went over to the school and dealt with Skeezer. What a mistake that turned out to be.

"Now there's no guarantee, but I think I see a trend here. According to my analysis—based on past performance—we should be happy again real soon. Hey, it's summer, you guys. How bad can it be?"

"I'll show you how bad it can be," Taylor said. "Hand over that chalk. There's more than one way of looking at things. I'm going to graph out my hideous thoughts per hour."

Often the axes will show not the actual numbers but a **scale** of the actual numbers. For example, a graph might show the hours of the day, and the *thousands* of times Taylor thought depressing thoughts.

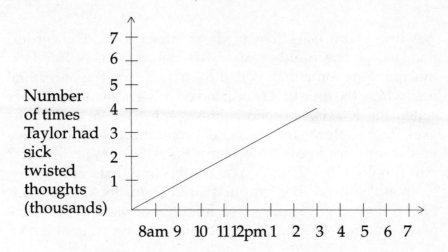

The graph above shows that at 3 p.m., Taylor thought horrible things not 4 times but 4,000 times.

To make your own line graph, draw 2 lines on a piece of paper. Then label the axes. For instance, how about a height graph for yourself, from age 5 to age 12 (or whatever age you are now)? Make the horizontal line "age" and the vertical "height," because height is vertical.

Now, starting with 5, put your age in years at equal distances apart on that line. Then, put inches on the other axis, starting below your height at age 5, to make it look good.

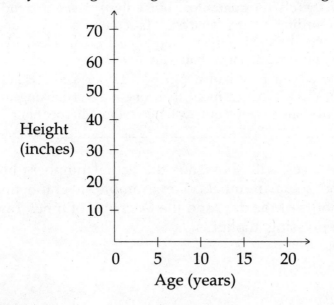

Now you can plot points. That means mark on the graph your height at each age. The person whose heights we are graphing was 30 inches tall at age 5, 32 inches at 6, 36" at 7, 38" at 8, 40" at 9, 42" at 10, 45" at 11, and 50" at 12.

To plot your own points, first go to the age. Then, look to the left axis for the corresponding height. Mark the intersection of height and age with a dark point.

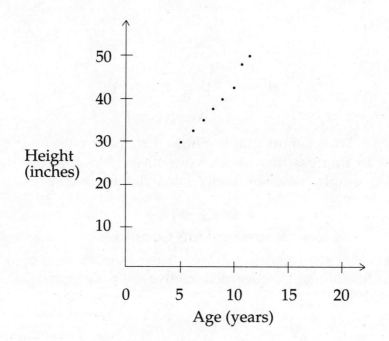

Do this with all of the measurements, then join the points with a line.

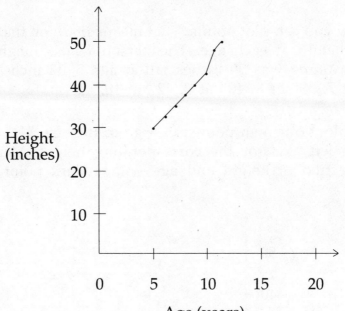

Voila! Your height graph. Show it to your parents if you want to impress them with your incredible growth—their height graphs have probably been flat for years.

✍ QUIZ #16 ✍
Reading Line Graphs

Look at the following graph of the number of people in Smalltown who learned to dive over the years 1985 to 1994.

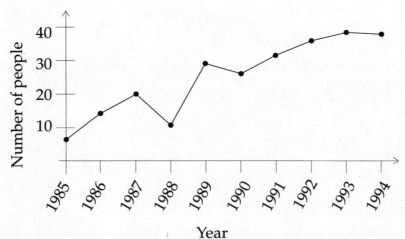

1. How many people in Smalltown learned to dive in 1987?

2. In what year did the greatest number of people learn to dive?

3. In what year did the fewest number of people learn to dive?

4. Between which two years was there the greatest increase in the number of people who learned to dive?

5. Between which two years was the greatest decrease in the number of people who learned to dive?

✎　✎　✎　✎　✎

"Hey, wait a minute, I want to make a graph too. I don't like these line graphs. Too dull. Here's a cool graph," Jennifer said, and she bent down and began to draw little pictures. "That's how many slices of pizza I ate, how many slices of blueberry pie, and how many hot dogs."

A **pictograph** represents information with little pictures. For these, it is important to know exactly what each picture indicates. This is usually done with a key or scale near the graph.

You can make your own pictograph. For instance, you might want to demonstrate where water for swimming is most plentiful in your neighborhood. First, decide on a scale.

Here we will use a scale in which each symbol represents 100 gallons. Think of a picture for each location, and approximate or figure out how many gallons each water source contains. Here's how it might look if you'd thought of three sources of water: a bathtub, a backyard pool, and a big duck pond.

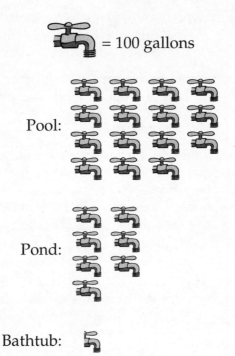

Pool:

Pond:

Bathtub:

This way you can show how things are relative to each other, you can use cool graphics, and you can get actual numbers from looking at the graph.

✍ QUIZ #17 ✍
Reading Pictographs

Look at the following graph of the number of people who listen to music in Smalltown. Each figure represents 100 people.

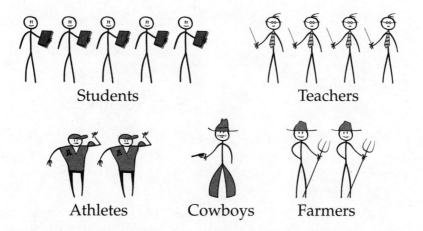

Students   Teachers

Athletes   Cowboys   Farmers

1. How many total farmers in Smalltown like to listen to music?

2. How many teachers in Smalltown like to listen to music?

3. Do more teachers or farmers in Smalltown like to listen to music?

4. In Smalltown, do more professional athletes or more cowboys like to listen to music?

5. In Smalltown, which group represented has the greatest number of people who like to listen to music?

✎ ✎ ✎ ✎ ✎

Taylor was studying Jennifer's pictograph when Sondra pulled Jennifer aside. "Speaking of pies..." she said.

Soon the two girls were busy making another graph and laughing while they did it. Taylor came over to investigate.

On the ground at his feet was drawn a circular chart:

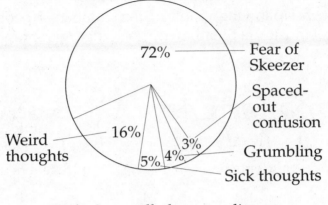

Taylor's so-called personality

A pictograph doesn't always give you a sense of the whole. How many people live in Smalltown, anyway? Well, we don't know. But Taylor's personality is seen, by Jennifer and Sondra at least, as a whole, and a **circle graph** represents how that whole is divided. A circle graph, also known as a pie chart, is just like that pizza we were cutting up in chapter 3, except that the pieces aren't so nice and even. That's why they are represented as percentages. In the girls' circle graph you can see that 72% of Taylor's personality has been taken up with his fear of Skeezer. Of course Sondra and Jennifer are just teasing Taylor; it really isn't possible to put exact numbers to a personality.

If you know exactly what the whole is, a circle graph can help you figure out the value of each piece of the graph. For instance, let's say Taylor has exactly 100 units of personality. If we know that 72% of his personality was used up on fear of Skeezer, then we know that 72 units of his personality have been used up. People often use circle graphs to keep track of expenditures; circle graphs allow you to see relative amounts of a whole very easily.

✍ QUIZ #18 ✍
Reading Pie Charts

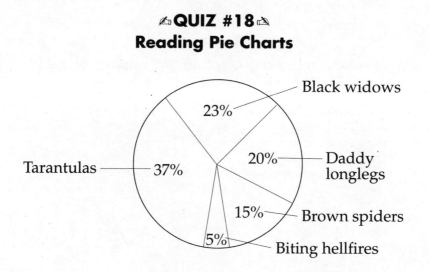

1. Are there more daddy longlegs or black widow spiders in the collection?

2. Are there more brown spiders or tarantulas in the collection?

3. If there are 100 spiders in the collection, how many spiders in the collection are black widows?

4. If there are 100 spiders in the collection, how many spiders in the collection are daddy longlegs?

5. If there are 100 spiders in the collection, how many of the spiders are *not* tarantulas?

✎ ✎ ✎ ✎ ✎

Sondra studied the various charts drawn on the ground for a moment, then said, "Okay, I've made up my mind. I know what we've got to do."

"Tell us, O Mighty Leader!" Taylor said, stretched out in his usual position among the roots.

"We're going swimming, that's all there is to it. We're going swimming, or this day is a total loss."

Review

Look at the following graph of the number of people who could Hula-Hoop in Smalltown.

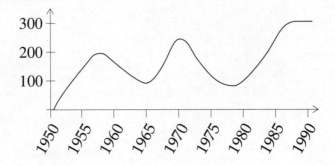

1. Approximately how many people could Hula-Hoop in 1965?

2. Approximately how many people could Hula-Hoop in 1972?

3. What was the year in which the greatest number of people could Hula-Hoop?

4. Between which two years was there the greatest increase in the number of people who could Hula-Hoop?

Sondra created this graph:

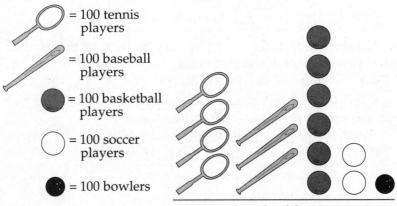

People who like coconut

5. Approximately how many bowlers like coconut?

6. Approximately how many tennis players like coconut?

7. What is the approximate difference between the number of basketball players who like coconut and the number of bowlers who like coconut?

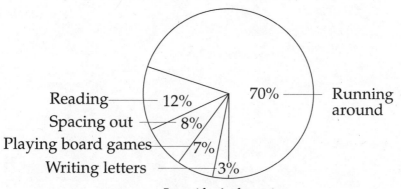

Jennifer's free time

8. Does Jennifer spend more time reading or spacing out in an average week?

9. If Jennifer has 50 hours of free time a week, how much time does she spend reading?

10. If Jennifer has 50 hours of free time per week, how much time does she spend playing board games and writing letters together?

✎ ✎ ✎ ✎ ✎

"Yeah, swimming," said Jennifer. "I mean, other people do it, *right*?"

"That's it!" yelled Sondra. "That's the spirit. I've got it! We'll go swimming at the country club!"

"But you need one of those special secret passes to go there," said Taylor, as Sondra and Jennifer scampered off toward the country club. "We won't get in, we'll never get in. Oh, here we go again."

Chapter 8
Geometry

The country club had wide green manicured lawns that rolled gently down to the central clubhouse. Surrounding these lawns were tall shady woods through which curved well-kept footpaths. From the golf course, beyond the woods and to the left, came the occasional faint cry of "Fore!" From the right came the steady *thwack* of tennis balls being slammed back and forth across the net. The kids crept along stealthily, as if they were thieves, though the only thing they were stealing was the view. The drifting scent of chlorine found their noses and they followed it down a trail through the thin woods.

As they entered a clearing, they heard the unmistakable sounds of splashing and laughter, followed by a lifeguard's shrill whistle. They hurried on a few more yards . . . then they saw it . . . a beautiful pool, shimmering in the sun like a turquoise jewel. They could see all the people inside: guys with skinny red legs, fluffy white chest hair, and

bellies that hung down over the elastic of their plaid bathing suits; girls lying on great big floral towels reading great big books; old ladies with wobbly arms rubbing suntan gook on their shoulders; college guys pushing each other around like they were fighting when really they were just showing off their muscles; a kid cannonballing off the high board who sent up a huge plume of spray that just barely missed the lifeguard. Of course, the lifeguard's nose was coated with that weird white lifeguard nose goop.

"Wow, incredible!" breathed Jennifer.

"We have to get in there," said Sondra. "No matter what it takes."

"Okay, sure, we'll just charm them with our good looks," Taylor said.

"What we need are passes. A couple of passes and we're all set."

"Well, I have construction paper," said Sondra. "Let's go get a look at those passes and copy them."

"Forge documents?" Taylor whispered passionately. "Sondra, I'm *amazed* at you. That's a federal offense. We could get the *electric couch.*"

"Taylor, you mean the *electric chair,*" Jennifer informed him.

"But there's three of us, so they'd have to use an *electric couch,*" Taylor snickered.

"You are so sick."

"Not at all, my *ideas* are sick. I am . . ."

"Really, really sick," Jennifer interrupted, "You are sick and *annoying*. I've put up with you all day, and Buster, I've had it up to here. Now we're going to get into that pool and go swimming, *right*? You're going to go along with everything Sondra and I say, *right*? And when we're swimming happily, leaping and diving and frolicking like fish, then you'll thank us, *right*? Because if you don't, I'm going to drown you. *Right*?"

"Okay, sure, whatever you say, Sarge. But . . . when we're frying on the electric couch, you remember who warned you."

"You will be extremely lucky to live that long."

"Alright, break it up you two. We're friends, remember?" Sondra jumped between Jennifer and Taylor. "Let's cool off our heads in that pool. Let's make those pool passes."

Jennifer went off to investigate while Sondra and Taylor hid in the shade of a tree near the fence that surrounded the pool. They looked longingly at the bright blue water. Before they knew it, Jennifer had returned.

"It's a red, star-shaped pass. Here, I'll draw it," she said. She took a stick and traced this figure in the dirt:

"We'll never be able to make that!" said Sondra. "Our construction paper is only in squares, and we don't have any scissors."

"I think we can make it anyway," said Jennifer. "I'll show you."

How can Jennifer make a star shape without cutting or tearing a square sheet of paper? Well, first it is important to know what shapes are made of. The outlines of shapes are made of **line segments**. Here are some line segments:

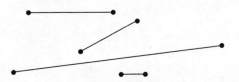

Why are these called line segments instead of **lines**? Because lines, in math language, go on forever. This is usually indicated by an arrow at either end, meaning the line just goes and goes and goes. Here is a line:

If you see something that looks like a line but only goes forever in one direction, that is a **ray**.

Many geometric shapes are made of straight line segments, for instance, **squares**, like the construction paper the kids have:

or **triangles**.

In fact, most of these shapes with straight sides can be made up of each other. For instance, a square is also two triangles next to each other.

A square can be folded in half to form a triangle.

And three triangles can be layered together to form a star, which is exactly what Jennifer did.

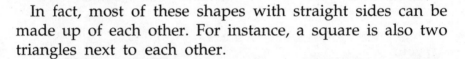

"Wait just a second," said Taylor. "I've seen those passes before. The club pass has a picture of the pool, a diamond, and a beach ball on it—in pen or something. We have to make sure ours are exactly the same, or we'll be frying."

"Then everybody just move aside," said Sondra, "and allow me to create my art." Sondra was often quite pleased with her drawings and didn't really mind letting everybody know it.

Here is what the interior design looked like:

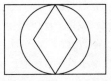

The pool is a **rectangle**, the beach ball is a **circle**, and the diamond is, you guessed it, a **diamond**.

The rectangle and diamond (the fancy name for a diamond is a **parallelogram**) are made with straight lines. To form line segments into these shapes, you make the line segments meet. The exact place where line segments (or lines) meet is called the **intersection**. When line segments intersect, **angles** are formed. An angle is the meeting of two lines or line segments. When you have a whole shape put together—the pool rectangle, for instance—the angles within the shape are called **vertices** (the fancy name for corners), or if it's only one corner you are talking about, a **vertex**. The space between vertices on a shape is called the **side**.

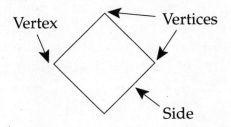

Flat shapes, such as circles and squares, are called **two-dimensional.** They are called two-dimensional because they have length and width (two dimensions), but no thickness.

What about a line segment? A line segment has length, but how much width does it have? Well, if you were to draw a line segment with a very thin pencil you might say that the line segment was too thin to measure, thinner than the smallest marks on a ruler. But it would still have *some* small thickness wouldn't it? That's because it exists in the real world; after all, you drew it. For mathematicians though, that line segment you drew only represents the *idea* of a line, the same way that the word *chair* represents the idea of a chair, but isn't a chair itself. You can't sit on the word *chair* (or if you did, it wouldn't be very comfortable). So a line segment, to a mathematician, is really the idea of a line segment; it has no width at all. It is a one-dimensional shape. Pretty crazy right?

Well, here's something even crazier. A **point.** A point looks like a dot. To mathematicians a point is very weird little dot though. *It has no dimensions at all.* No height, length, or thickness. A point indicates a place, but, on its own, a point doesn't exist at all. The real world doesn't have objects like these in it, with only zero, one, or two dimensions. If you examined a dot with a microscope you'd discover that it definitely has dimensions, even thickness.

The real world is made of **three-dimensional** shapes. Three-dimensional things take up space, or what mathematicians call **volume.** Imagine a flat uninflated raft. The raft should be so flat it has no thickness at all, *none.* That's probably pretty hard to imagine since such an object would be physically impossible, but remember, that's how mathematicians think of two-dimensional space, as absolutely without thickness. If you then puff up that raft with breath, it takes up space. You are giving it volume by filling it with air from your lungs.

An inflated circle would form a **sphere**, like the globe or a gumball.

Or, if the circle just inflated upward so it looked like a can of soup, it would be a **cylinder**.

A **cone** is a shape that tapers evenly from a circle down to a single point. It looks like what might happen if a circle and a triangle had a three-dimensional child. (A witch's hat without the wide brim is a cone.)

What would an inflated square look like? It's a **cube**. Dice are cubes, sometimes sugar comes in cubes, and some people like to cut cheese into tiny cubes.

A good way to draw a cube, if you're interested, is to draw two equal squares overlapping just a little bit. Then, draw line segments to join the vertices.

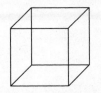

Ta da! You're an artist. Try shading your drawing different ways. It's interesting to see how the same basic shape can seem to be in different positions.

✎ ✎ ✎ ✎ ✎

"You know, I've heard they quiz you if they so much as suspect you have a fake pass," said Taylor.

"That isn't true!" cried Jennifer. "Is it?"

"I've heard the same thing," Sondra admitted. "Maybe we should prepare a little?"

Jennifer looked concerned. "What sort of things do they ask?"

"Oh, things like how many square feet is the surface of the pool, you know, stuff you would know if you came here a lot," said Sondra.

What are **square feet**? They are squares that have sides measuring 1 foot each. And **square inches** are squares that have sides measuring 1 inch each. These type of square measurements are how people measure flat surfaces. A large handkerchief is almost exactly 1 square foot.

✎ ✎ ✎ ✎ ✎

"What other kinds of questions do they ask? This whole quiz idea is making me nervous," said Jennifer.

"Well, they might ask if that weird marble design on the bottom of the pool is really a square, and what other shapes are in it," said Sondra.

"Well, is it a square?" shrieked Jennifer. "I don't know any of this stuff!"

"Relax," said Sondra. "I came here once with a friend's family and I saw the whole design. I can draw it for you in the dirt and you can see the whole thing. But first I'll show you the square thing."

Some of the things that make squares square are its angles. Angles are measured in degrees. A flat line has exactly 180 degrees, which would be written like this: 180°. The small circle just after the 0 is the degree symbol.

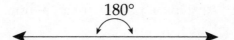

All four of a square's angles must be **right angles**, which means that they must be exactly equal halves of a straight line. Right angles have exactly 90°. When a straight line intersects another straight line, and divides the angle of that straight line exactly in half, right angles are formed. When two lines meet this way and form right angles, these lines are called **perpendicular**. Right angles are labeled in math by a tiny square in the vertex of the angle.

When *lines* never **intersect**, they are called **parallel**. They stay an equal distance apart no matter how long they go on. The symbol to show that lines are parallel is this: $l_1 \parallel l_2$.

It's important to remember that just because two line *segments* don't intersect doesn't mean they're parallel. If you want to know if two line segments are parallel they have to be extended to infinity—that is, turned into *lines*. If they would ever touch when extended, then the line segments are not parallel.

Once you have intersecting lines and parallel lines, you have almost all the tools you need to draw your own figures. To draw lines, all you need to do is create two points and connect them. Any two points form a line.

Here is the design on the bottom of the pool that the kids need to know about. Can you identify the shapes used to create it?

The shapes here are **planar**, or two-dimensional. Both these words are used to describe a shape as flat. The way to identify most closed planar geometric shapes is to count the number of sides. The outside shape is called an **octagon**; octo, as in octopus, as in eight sides. The shape just inside it is called a **hexagon**; that means it has six sides. Within that is a **pentagon**; penta means five, like the Pentagon building which houses the United States Department of Defense. Inside the pentagon is a **quadrilateral**; quad means four. Notice that none of these shapes requires right angles or equal sides. A square is a quadrilateral:

But this is also a quadrilateral:

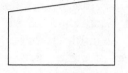

If you see two figures or angles that are the exact same size and shape, they are said to be **congruent**. Congruent means identical in size and shape. These two quadrilaterals are congruent:

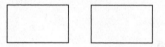

These two are not:

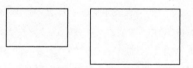

What if you were to draw a line that went from one corner of a rectangle to the opposite corner, right through the center, like this:

Such a line would be called a **diagonal**.

Then, of course, at the center is a plain old circle. One way to draw a circle is to take a small piece of string or wire and place one end of it in the middle of a sheet of paper. Put your pencil or pen point at the other end of the string and, while pressing that other end down toward the center, run your pencil all the way around it at the greatest length of the wire you can. You should end up with a perfect circle.

✎ ✎ ✎ ✎ ✎

"Okay, so now I can identify all the dumb things in their pool, but I'm still nervous," said Jennifer. "I don't trust any of this stuff. I wish there were some other way to go swimming. Oh yeah, and what about that other question, about the square feet of the pool? How are we ever going to find out how many square feet the pool takes up?"

"That shouldn't be so hard," said Sondra. "There are racing markers along the outside every ten yards. The way I count it, the pool is fifty yards long. And it looks about twice as long as it is wide. So it's twenty-five yards wide."

"So? That still doesn't tell us the number of square feet."

"Oh yes, it does," Sondra said.

The number of square feet a surface occupies, or the amount of square yards of fabric needed to make a tablecloth, or carpet to cover a floor, or . . . okay, you get the idea; all those things are found by getting the **area** of that shape. Area tells us how many square units— square feet, or inches, or yards, or meters, or miles, or any other unit of distance—a shape occupies. For any rectangle (including squares), in this case a swimming pool, the area is found by multiplying the **length** of the shape by its **width**.

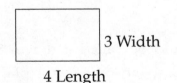

3 Width

4 Length

Since the rectangle above has length of 4 and a width of 3, the area of that rectangle is 12, 4 × 3 = 12. The length of a rectangle is its longer side, and the width is its shorter side. Some people also call these **dimensions** of a shape. Dimensions means measurements, the **base** and **height**. The height of any planar geometric shape is the length of a line that forms a right angle when drawn from its highest point to its base.

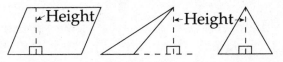

So the swimming pool was 50 yards long by 25 yards wide. How many square yards is that? Okay, now remember the kids wanted to know how many square *feet* there are in the pool. How would you figure that out? Careful, it's a super-tricky question.

Did you think that you would multiply the number of square yards by three since there are three feet in every one yard? If you thought that, you fell for the trick. Look at this drawing:

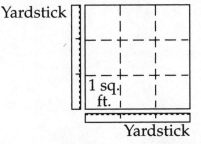

You see, there are nine square feet in one square yard. A **linear** yard (linear means "along a line") contains three linear feet. But a square yard contains nine square feet. Why? Because we **squared** three. A number is squared when it is multiplied by itself. 3 times 3 is 9; 3 squared is 9. 5 times 5 is 25; 5 squared is 25. Pretty simple, right?

The mathematical symbol for squaring is a small number two written above and to the right of a digit. For example 3 squared is written by mathematicians like this 3^2. The small two there is called an **exponent**. It tells you to multiply 3 by itself 2 times. Remember, that *doesn't* mean 3 × 2. It means 3 × 3.

How about 4^3? Can you guess what that means? It means 4 × 4 × 4. Four times itself three times, *not* 4 × 3. How about 3^3? That means 3 × 3 × 3. Numbers with exponents attached to them can become tricky to work with. For now, you should recognize them and know what they mean.

So is any of this making you think about the relationship between a rectangle and a square? A square is just a rectangle with four equal sides. To find the area of a square you multiply the length times the width. Because all the sides of a square are equal the length and width are equal. So the same number is multiplied by itself.

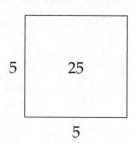

Both squares and rectangles are special kinds of quadrilaterals called **parallelograms**. A parallelogram is a quadrilateral in which opposite sides are parallel.

If, instead of finding the area of one of these shapes, you wanted to figure out how many inches of string it would take to wrap its edges, that measure would be called the **perimeter**. The perimeter is the length of the outside border of a shape.

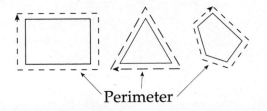

Perimeter

To find the perimeter, just add up the sides of a figure.

What if you wanted to measure the angles of a shape? You can do this too. For instance, say you wanted the area of a shape like this:

But before finding the area, you wanted to make sure it was a square. If the shape is a square, the area is easy, just length times width, or since in a square these are equal, one of the sides, squared. To find out, you need to see if the angles are right angles, and to do this you need a **protractor**. A protractor looks like this:

To protract something means to make it longer. A protractor can lengthen the line segments that create an angle. You already know that angles are made of degrees. To find out how many degrees a specific angle has, line the bottom of the protractor up with one of the lines that make up the angle, then look to where the other line of the angle falls.

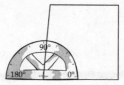

This protractor shows that our shape is, in fact, not a square. This angle is 100°, not 90°. You can measure the other angles of this shape with your own protractor. But no matter what, those four angles will add up to 360°, because all quadrilaterals have degrees adding up to 360.

What about triangles? Well, if you cut any quadrilateral in half, you make two triangles.

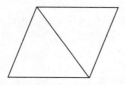

So, how many degrees do you think a triangle has? A triangle has 180°, half of 360°.

What about a circle? Take a look. First look at a circle with a line drawn through the center. In a circle this line is not called a diagonal, it is called a **diameter**. A diameter is a line in a circle that goes through the center.

Diameter

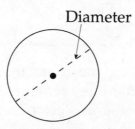

Since each side of a straight line is an angle of 180°, and there are two sides of the straight line forming the diameter, all circles have two times 180°, or 360°.

The center of a circle is the point exactly in the middle, meaning the point that is of equal distance from all the edges of the circle. If you draw a line from the center to any point on the edge of the circle, that line is called a **radius**.

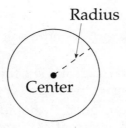

The outer edge of a circle is called the **circumference**. But the word for how much surface a circle covers is still "area."

The only other words you need to know are those for three-dimensional shapes. The flat surfaces of three-dimensional shapes are called **faces**; the lines that make up the sides are called **edges**; and the corners, like the corners of other shapes, are called **vertices**.

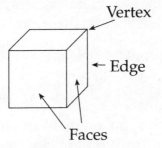

"We are totally doomed to suffer and suffer and never go swimming. These construction paper passes aren't going to work. They're so ridiculous we won't even be executed, we'll just be laughed at. How humiliating. Let's throw sand in our eyes. It's a lot more fun," Taylor said dramatically.

"Well," said Jennifer, looking at the passes and thinking about the quiz, "maybe the front gate isn't such a great idea after all . . . . Maybe there's another way!"

"And what way would that be?" asked Taylor.

"You see that tree? Maybe we could climb up it and just drop over this darn fence into the club without ever going near the front gate!"

"I don't know," said Taylor. "We're pretty small, and that's a pretty big tree."

"And I'm a pretty girl," Sondra said, "so *I* should have no trouble at all."

Jennifer and Taylor each stuck a finger in their mouths and made horrible gagging sounds.

"Well, if the angle is good it shouldn't be any problem at all," Jennifer looked up at the tree, then back to the sparkling blue pool.

What angle is easiest for climbing a tree? Well, not a right angle certainly, a right angle would mean you had to climb straight up. But an **acute** angle might be just the thing. An acute angle is an angle of less than 90°. These are all acute angles, and if you imagine them as trees leaning over a fence, you can see how easy it might be to climb them:

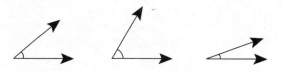

The opposite of an acute angle is an **obtuse** angle, the sort you don't want in a tree you are climbing. An obtuse angle is one greater than 90°. These angles are all obtuse:

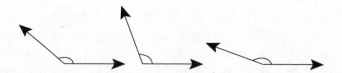

Angles like these often make up special types of triangles. A triangle with three equal sides also has three equal angles— acute angles, as you can see—and is called an **equilateral triangle**.

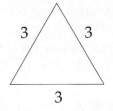

When a triangle has two equal sides, which also means it has two equal angles, it is called an **isosceles triangle**.

The isosceles triangle that is furthest to the right has a right angle, which means it is not only an isosceles triangle but a **right triangle**. A right triangle is a triangle which includes a right angle.

When you find triangles, or quadrilaterals for that matter, with identical sides and angles you know they are called congruent. But there is another way shapes can be compared. For instance, if two triangles have equal angles and sides that are in the same ratio, these triangles are called **similar**. These two triangles are similar.

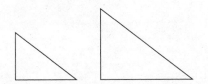

All circles are similar, because they are simply the same shape with the same number of degrees, made larger or smaller. And circles have their own special interior ratio. What if you measured the outside, or circumference, of a circle and compared that measurement to its diameter? You will find that the circumference is always a little bit more than three times the diameter. The relationship between these two measurements—the ratio between them—is called **pi**. Pronounced "pie," as in blueberry pie. It is a Greek letter and it looks like this: π. The value of π is approximately 3.14, though the actual exact value goes on forever and ever, an infinite decimal. So if you know the diameter of a circle and you want to know the circumference, just multiply the diameter by 3.14. And if you know the circumference and you want to know the diameter, just divide the circumference by 3.14.

APPROXIMATE THIS

How many grooves are on the circumference of a dime?

✎ ✎ ✎ ✎ ✎

"See, here is the tree and we'll just shinny up and drop down from this overhanging branch here, alright?" said Jennifer. She drew Taylor a diagram of the tree in the dirt and showed him how they would climb. "Here's where we would drop off," she said.

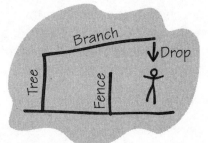

"That would work!" said Taylor excitedly.

"*What* would work, young man?" said a deep voice.

Jennifer and Taylor turned to see the large, disapproving face of one of the country club security guards.

"Um, nothing, nothing would work," said Jennifer.

"I asked you a question, young man," the guard said to Taylor. "*What* would work?"

"I just meant that either of these could be changed to form a rhombus or a trapezoid," said Taylor, thinking fast.

"A what who?" said the guard, completely befuddled.

A **rhombus** is a parallelogram with four equal sides. It looks like a squished square. Taylor changed the diagram so it looked like this:

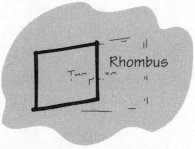

A **trapezoid** is a figure in which two of the sides are parallel and two are not. Taylor changed to the diagram to look like this:

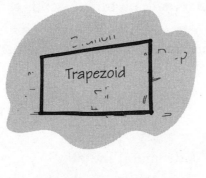

"You're having your geometry lesson up here under this tree then?" asked the guard (who had lots of thick black hair growing out of his ears) suspiciously. "Interesting place to choose for summer school."

"Well, mumblemumble *ear hair* mumble," Taylor said, smiling.

"Ear hair? Whatta you mean, ear hair?"

"Ear hair? I didn't say that. I said *air here*, that's why we're having our geometry lessons under this tree, because of the *air here*. Maybe you don't hear so well? Maybe you ought to have your ears checked?"

"*Maybe* you'd better just come with me to the main office."

"You don't believe we were doing geometry at all, do you, Mr. Guard?" Sondra said, jumping in.

"Well, we were," Jennifer said before the guard could say anything. "We were and we can prove it. Take a look at those tables down there by the pool. We'll tell you what the area of any of them is, or the perimeter. Whatever you want to know."

The country club had all sorts of tables—rectangles, squares, triangles, circles, trapezoids, and parallelograms. Jennifer knew that rectangles and squares both have areas that can be found by multiplying length times width for the rectangle, and side times side for the square. (Does it make more sense now why multiplying something times itself is called "squaring"?)

But how about triangles? Since the area of a rectangle is length times width, look again at one way triangles are formed.

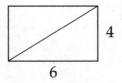

By cutting a quadrilateral in half. So the area of a triangle is half the area of a quadrilateral. The area of a triangle is one-half of the base times the height, also known as b × h. The area of one of the triangles in the figure above is 12, while the area of the whole rectangle is 24. Remember, the height of the triangle must form a perpendicular to the base or it isn't the height.

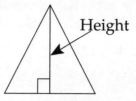

Height

The area of a parallelogram is simple once you have the perpendicular height. Then the area can be found by base times height, just as it can with any other quadrilateral.

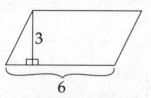

3

6

The area of the parallelogram above is 18.

A trapezoid is a bit trickier. The area of a trapezoid is one-half the sum of the parallel sides times the height.

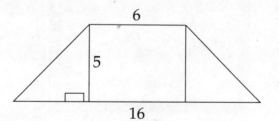

6

5

16

The area of the trapezoid above is 55 square units.

A circle's surface area can be found by multiplying π by the square of the radius. Also known as πr^2.

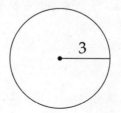

3

The area of the circle above is 9π. To find the circumference, multiply π times the diameter. Or, since the radius is half the diameter, multiply π by the radius times two. These two ways are the same thing. Also known as πd or $2\pi r$. The circumference of the previous circle is 6π.

✎ ✎ ✎ ✎ ✎

The guard looked at the three kids and shook his head. "Nope, I don't want to know the area of any of those tables. What I've wondered about for years is how much water fills that pool. Must be an awful lot. So tell me, what's the volume of the pool?" The guard crossed his arms over his chest, looking very pleased with himself. They'll never get it, he thought.

Finding the volume of a rectangular space is a lot like finding the area. The pool, on the surface, is 25 yards by 50 yards.

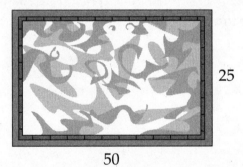

25

50

So its surface area is 1,250 square yards. To find the volume, just multiply those first two dimensions by the third dimension, the depth. Luckily, this pool has no deep or shallow end, it is all 2 yards deep.

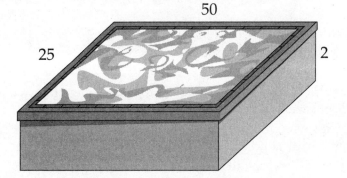

Volume is length times width times depth, or, V = l × w × d.

$$50 \times 25 \times 2 = 2{,}500$$

There are 2,500 cubic yards of water in the pool.

✎ ✎ ✎ ✎ ✎

"2,500 cubic yards," shouted Jennifer.

The guard said, "That's pretty good . . . you kids are pretty good. I've been wondering about that question for years now and nobody ever told me. You know what I'm going to do?"

"Sure, we know exactly what you're going to do. You're going to let us in to go swimming for free, *right*?" Jennifer said.

"You're going to give us free passes to the pool for the whole summer!" Sondra gasped.

"Hooray, for the pool guard!" Taylor shouted. "I can't believe something actually worked out!"

"No, no, I'm sorry kids," the guard said. "I can't let you into the pool for free. It's against the club rules. But I am going to overlook the fact that you're trespassing and just let you go with a warning." And with that the guard walked off, humming to himself.

"Thanks for nothing, Ear-hair," Jennifer said after the guard had left.

"You know what I was just thinking about adults?" Taylor said.

"No," Sondra said.

"Well, they're older than we are."

"Really?"

"So most likely they're going to die sooner than we are, and that seems like a good thing," Taylor said thoughtfully.

"That was our only real chance to swim!" Jennifer said in a tearful voice.

"I've given up all hope too," Sondra groaned.

"Let's get out of here," said Taylor.

They started walking away, past the gate that surrounded the country club, along the edge where you could see everyone splashing happily in the pool, by the landscaped bushes and trees where a bunch of people stood pointing up at the top of the biggest tree.

"What's going on?" said Jennifer.

"Who cares what's going on at this lousy country club?" said Sondra, "Let's just go."

But they heard people saying, "Call Larry's Ladders!" and "No, find our own ladder!"

"What's going on?" Jennifer called over the fence.

The guard, the one with the yucky, hairy ears they'd just been talking to, pointed up. "There's a huge black cat stuck up in the tree, and we can't mess up the hedges because they're Mrs. Beardsly's, and Larry's Ladders will cost tons of money but we don't know if our ladder is long enough!"

The kids looked nervously up at the cat in the tree. . . . It was Beauregard. He smiled down at them, winked, then let out a long pitiful howl.

"Oh the poor kitty, it's terrified, oh my," a few bystanders murmured. "Do something! Quick!"

"Geez," the guard said. "If I tear up Mrs. Beardsly's hedges, I'll lose my job. And if I use club money to buy one of Larry's ladders when it isn't necessary, I'll lose my job. And if I don't get that cat out of that tree pretty quick, I'll lose my job."

"Sure would hate to see that," Jennifer said.

"Yep, a crying shame," Taylor piped in.

"Of course, using geometry *could* tell you what to do. How long is the country club ladder?" Sondra asked.

"Fifteen feet," said the guard.

"If we let you know whether it's long enough, can we all get in for free?" Taylor asked.

"Kid, if you let me know that, you and your friends here can get in free for the rest of the summer!" said the guard.

The kids used the **Pythagorean Theorem**. They saw that using the ladder would form a big triangle, and since the tree was pretty much straight up from the ground, it would be a right triangle. The Pythagorean Theorem says that for any right triangle, the square of the two shorter sides added together will equal the square of the longest side. The longest side, also known as the **hypotenuse**, is the side opposite the right angle. Here the hypotenuse will be the ladder. The shorter sides of a right triangle are also known as the **legs**. So for a right triangle like this:

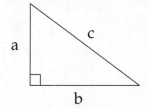

The formula is $a^2 + b^2 = c^2$. If you had a right triangle with legs of 3 and 4, it would be easy to figure out the third side.

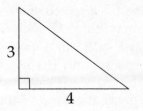

Add the square of the legs.

$3^2 + 4^2 = c^2$

$9 + 16 = c^2$

$25 = c^2$

What squared equals 25? Five, so the third side is 5.

Since Jennifer approximated the height and base of the triangle formed by the tree and the hedges, she could figure out the length of the ladder needed. She looked at the tree and saw it was about 12 feet tall, because it was twice as tall as her father, who is 6 feet tall. She looked at the hedges and saw they were as tall as she would be if she were lying down; in other words, 5 feet tall. So what was the third side?

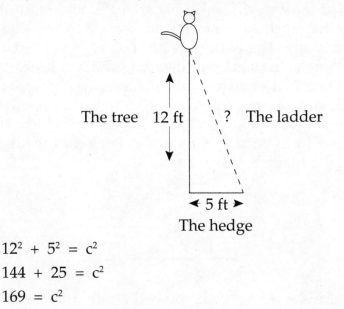

The tree   12 ft   ?   The ladder

◄ 5 ft ►

The hedge

$12^2 + 5^2 = c^2$

$144 + 25 = c^2$

$169 = c^2$

What squared is equal to 169? Well, it must be bigger than 12, because 12 squared is only 144, so try the next biggest whole number, 13. And that's it, 13 times 13 is 169. So the club's 15-foot ladder is tall enough.

✎ ✎ ✎ ✎ ✎

"Your ladder is long enough. Just run and get it and you can, uh, rescue that poor, terrified kitty cat," Jennifer said.

"Great!" said the guard. "And you kids just come around the front and come right in. Swim as much as you like." The guard ran off to get the ladder.

As soon as the guard was gone, Beauregard hopped gracefully out of the tree, pulled out a bottle of fur-tan lotion, popped on a pair of sunglasses, and said, "Kitty cat? I get you all free passes into the country club pool and that's the thanks I get. Goodness."

"Sorry, Beauregard," Jennifer said.

"Oh, don't worry at all, I was only teasing. But quick, let's get to the pool before that guard comes back and tries to rescue me. Imagine *him* rescuing *me*."

They headed straight for the pool.

✐ **QUIZ #20** ✐
Review

1. What is this shape?

2. What is the name of this shape?

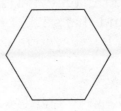

3. What is the line that passes through the center of a circle?

4. Approximate how many degrees are in this angle.

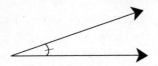

Is it obtuse, acute, or right?

5. What is the volume of this rectangular solid?

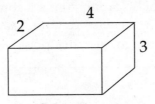

6. Sondra is painting a line around the edge of her carpet.

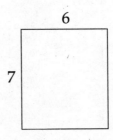

How long will the line be?

7. Taylor is trying to determine how many right angles are enclosed in this figure:

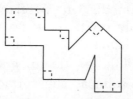

How many are there? (If an angle in this picture looks right, it is right.)

8. Jennifer wants to cut a piece of burlap to cover an ugly picture of a duck that her parents put on the wall of her bedroom. If the picture is a rectangle with a length of 3 feet and a width of 2 feet, how many square feet of burlap will she need?

9. Taylor is trying to describe the shape of a new sculpture his father made to a friend over the phone. This is the sculpture:

How should he describe it?

10. Sondra is carving a circular tray for her mother. If the tray is 4 feet across from edge to edge through the center, what is its measurement around the edge?

❧ ❧ ❧ ❧ ❧

Back at the pool, Jennifer bombed a cannonball into the water, Taylor swam the length of the pool underwater, Sondra dove primly off the low board, and Beauregard chatted with the lifeguard. The water was cool and blue.

"You know something?" Jennifer said.

"What?" said Sondra as she surfaced from a dive.

"I think she's going to say that it was all worth it," said Taylor.

"*Right,*" said Jennifer.

Chapter 9
Negative Numbers

The day wore on into the early evening as the three kids and the cat frolicked around the pool.

"Ahh, this is the life," Taylor said, dangling his feet over the sides of an inflatable raft. "Blue sky above and blue water below. Ahhh, at last nothing, but *nothing*, can go wrong."

The lifeguard blew her whistle, "Okay, closing time! Everybody out of the pool."

Everybody began swimming to the sides and climbing out of the pool, but Jennifer, Sondra, and Taylor were determined to be the last ones to leave. They wanted to stretch this out to the last minute. Finally, the lifeguard called out to them, "Alright you three, out of the pool!"

Sondra headed toward the edge doing the butterfly stroke. Taylor slowly paddled his raft toward the edge of the pool. But Jennifer said, "Hey, I wonder what would happen if . . ." and she ducked under the surface of the water.

Sondra had almost made it to the edge when, just as she reached for the ladder to climb out, she couldn't move. It felt as if she were being sucked backward. She *was* being sucked backward! Behind her she heard Taylor yelling, "Quick! Get out! Whirlpool!!! We're doomed . . . We're getting pulled down . . . I *knew* this would happen . . . AIEEEEEEEeeeeeeeeblblblbbbbbbbbb."

Sondra turned around. It was true. A whirlpool swirled at the center of the swimming pool—and it had Taylor. As she watched helplessly, Taylor's feet disappeared into the sucking hole of water. It had Sondra, too. The drag of the water held her like a huge hand. She couldn't get free. She swam against the current as hard as she could but it was useless; it had her and wouldn't let go. The whirlpool roared. Sondra was whipped round and round. She was pulled down the spinning tube of water at the whirlpool's heart.

"Taylor? Jennifer? Are you there? Are you alive?" Sondra called down into the pitch darkness. Her voice echoed gloomily off the walls of what must have been a large underground chamber. The thick, wet air smelled of mildew. The hard floor felt cold and slick. In the darkness she could hear water trickling over stone.

"I believe we're dead," Taylor's voice said calmly somewhere to Sondra's left.

"I guess I shouldn't have pulled out that plug," Sondra heard Jennifer say.

"You what?" Taylor's voice gasped.

"I wondered what would happen if I pulled the plug out from the bottom of the pool. I guess I found out. Sorry."

"We got sucked down the drain, didn't we?" Sondra exclaimed.

"Sucked down the drain! What a humiliating way to die!" Taylor yelled.

There was a tiny pinprick of light high above them. "That must be God," Taylor said. "I always heard when you died

God would appear as a bright light. Watch, it'll get larger and larger then we'll be flooded with feelings of peace and beauty, and then . . . actually, I don't know what happens after that . . ."

"Taylor, the light isn't changing, and it isn't all that bright either," Sondra said flatly. "And I don't think we're dead. I think we got sucked down the drain; that tiny dot of light is the hole we got sucked through."

"Great, so we're not even dead yet, we're just *going to die*," Taylor groaned.

Then, from high above, a familiar voice floated down to them "Jennnniiiiiffeeeer? Sooondraaa? Taaaaaylooor?"

"Beauregard!" the kids shouted. "Down here! We're okay!"

"Taaaaaylooor? Jennnniiiiiffeeeer? Sooondraaa?"

"Down here! We're okay!"

"Sooondraaa? Taaaaaylooor? Jennnnniiiiiffeeeer?"

"He can't hear us!"

"How?"

As their eyes adjusted to the darkness the kids began to look around at each other and the dim, vague shapes that surrounded them. They looked up at the far-off drainhole.

Quietly, Jennifer said, "I'm really sorry, guys."

"That's okay, Jenny," Sondra whispered.

"Yeah, don't worry about it, Jennifer, we're just going to die long, horrible, suffering deaths down here in the dark. No big deal."

"Stop it, Taylor!" Sondra screamed.

"No, it's true, he's right," Jennifer said sadly. "We're in big trouble and it's all my fault. I deserve it."

"No way. Who cares whose fault it is, let's just figure out a way to get back to the surface," Sondra was suddenly pragmatic, after being panic-stricken.

"I can tnell you how to gnet bnack to the snurface," a small voice in the darkness said.

"Who's there?" Jennifer called into the darkness.

"*Aaaaaaaaaaaaaaahhhhhhhhhhhh!*"

"Stop screaming, Sondra!" Jennifer said. "If something wanted to hurt us, it already would have."

"*I* wasn't screaming, that was *Taylor*."

"I snorry to alarmn you," the snuffling voice said, "bnut I couldn't help noticing the you were in trouble and I thnougnt I might be of nassisstance."

"Yes, please assist us. Get us out of here," Sondra said, a little bit rudely.

"Well, *I* can't gnet you out of here, bnut maybe I can help you find snomeone who can."

Straining their vision in the faint light, the kids could just barely make out the shape of a creature the size of a beagle, blob-like, waddling on four tiny, short legs.

"Who are you? *What* are you?" Taylor broke in.

"Allow me to nintrodnuce myself. I am Noel, the mole. The negativity mole."

"Phew," said Taylor. "I thought you were something weird, like a *ghost*."

"Okay Noel, take us to whoever it is can get us out of here," Jennifer said, "because I'm getting hungry."

"Wait a minute," Sondra said. "A negativity mole? I've never heard of that. Where are we?"

"Why, nyour below the snurface."

"Of the earth?"

"Not exnactly. You went through some kind of warp when you were snucked through the whirlpool of the drain. You're below the snurface of numbers. It happened to a kid a few years bnack. The sname way. I don't think she made it out, though I'm snure you'll do bnetter. Follow me."

Below the surface of numbers? What does Noel mean? He means **negative numbers**. Negative numbers are numbers smaller than zero. Remember the number line?

$$\xleftarrow{\hspace{0.5em}} \overset{\displaystyle -5 \quad -4 \quad -3 \quad -2 \quad -1 \quad 0 \quad 1 \quad 2 \quad 3 \quad 4 \quad 5}{\rule[0.5ex]{9cm}{0.4pt}} \xrightarrow{\hspace{0.5em}}$$

You've already learned about numbers to the right of zero. Numbers larger than zero are called **positive**. Numbers to the left of zero are negative, and the line extends to infinity in this direction as well. To think about negative and positive numbers, look at the number line this way:

$$
\begin{array}{c}
\uparrow \\
5 \\
4 \\
3 \\
2 \\
1 \\
0 \\
-1 \\
-2 \\
-3 \\
-4 \\
-5 \\
\downarrow
\end{array}
$$

Positive numbers here are above zero, and negative numbers are below zero. Think of zero as the level of flat ground, and the number line as a ladder dropping into negative numbers. Zero is neither positive nor negative. A good way to imagine negative and positive is as directions. Up is positive. Down is negative.

✎ ✎ ✎ ✎ ✎

"Come on," said Noel the mole as he led the kids along twisting tunnels on hands and knees through slimy crawlspaces where the air sometimes became hard to breathe. "Over here," Noel called, "and dnown this ladder ten rungs."

"But if we're already below the surface of numbers, we're just going farther down!" Sondra cried. "How far down are we now?"

"It doesn't mnatter. You're down so far I wouldn't neven worry about it. Just keep track of how far up and dnown we're going from here. If you must have a number to work with, call it one hnundred. You're one hnundred down."

"Where are you taking us?" Taylor wanted to know.

"Didn't I tnell you already? I'm taking you to Mr. X— he can help you. At least I hope so. Now hurry. Dnown the ladder."

The kids are at negative 100.

$$-50$$
$$-60$$
$$-70$$
$$-80$$
$$-90$$
$$-100$$

Now they go down 10 more. Where does going down 10 rungs put them?

On the number line it would look like this:

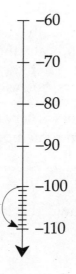

So the kids are down –110.

If you look on the number line, you will notice that –5 is below –3. This means –5 is actually smaller than –3. Think of the kids climbing down the ladder. They're at –110. What that means is 110 *down* from zero. In other words, –110 is a lot smaller than zero; –110 is smaller than 1, or –1. It's easy to get confused by negative numbers if you just look at the digits and forget about the negative sign, which means direction.

Another way you can think of negative numbers is with money. Would you rather owe someone 3 dollars or 500 dollars? Owing 3 dollars would be better, because it is easier to pay back. Owing money is like having negative money. If you have –3 dollars, you owe 3 dollars, and you are richer than if you have –500 dollars, which means you owe 500 dollars.

When in doubt, remember the number line or the kids in the hole. Whatever is closer to the surface, or higher up, is bigger.

THINK ABOUT THIS

Negative numbers are usually written with a minus sign in front of them to indicate they are negative; –5 is negative five. So why don't they have a plus sign in front of positive numbers, you ask? Well, they just don't.

Adding negative numbers is very similar to adding positive numbers. You just have to remember to include the negative sign.

$$-100 + -10 = -110$$

The kids go 10 feet down the ladder. You can look at it on the number line.

"Now, cnome non with me, hurry hurry," Noel urged. "We have to try and find Mr. X if you gnuys are ever going to get out of here. Onver here. Follow me, up this ladder seven rungs."

The kids are at –110 and they climb up 7. In other words, –110 + 7. Negatives go down, positives go up. What do you think happens? Watch on the number line.

–110 + 7 = –103. In other words, you take the difference between the two and keep the sign of the larger number. It could have just as easily been written like this: 7 – 110.

All that means is from positive 7 go *down* 110. Watch:

The answer is the same, –103. You get to the exact same place.

Let's practice these ideas with some smaller numbers. Let's add a positive number and a negative number.

4 – 2 = ? Hey, we said add a positive and a negative. This looks like regular old subtraction, and it is—it works the same way. From now on when you subtract, think of it as adding a positive and a negative. What is +4 and –2? 2 of course. Now let's try it the other way around. Positive 2 plus –4. That looks like this 2 – 4.

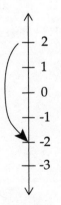

Simple right? When the signs are different, find the difference and keep the sign of the larger number. $2 - 4 = -2$

Look at the number line.

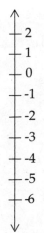

Starting from 2 above, you go *down* 4, which brings you to -2.

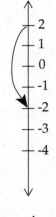

$$2 + -4 = -2$$

Of course, you can use your regular horizontal number line to do this for negative numbers; just start at the positive number and move to the left.

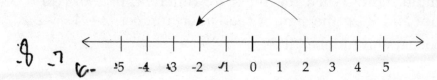

-8   -7   6-   -5   -4   3-   -2   1-   0   1   2   3   4   5

Okay, let's go deeper. –2 – 5 That means we start at –2 and go further in the same direction. We're still going down. Look at the number line.

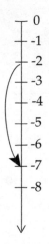

When the signs are the same, combine and keep the sign.

Now let's look at some weird ones. –6 minus –4 = ? Well, what would that mean? It would look like this: –6 – –4=? You are going back up toward the surface! To subtract a negative, go up. A way to remember this is to think of the two negative signs together forming a plus sign.

What's really happening is that the negative sign tells you what direction to go in. Two negatives in a row tell you to turn backward, then turn backward again. This works even if you are subtracting a negative from a positive. For instance:

$$7 - -3 = 10$$

$$7 - (\downarrow) - (\uparrow) 3 = 10$$
$$7 \quad + \quad 3 = 10$$

Another way negative numbers might pop up in your life is in regular subtraction with whole numbers. For example, if the temperature is 4°, and overnight it drops 5°, how cold is it? Take a look at the number line.

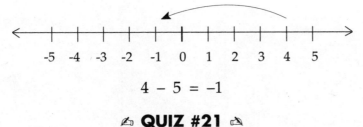

$$4 - 5 = -1$$

✍ QUIZ #21 ✍
Negative Numbers

1. Which is bigger, –5 or –7?

2. Which is bigger, –1 or 0?

3. Which is bigger, –13 or –31?

4. $-3 + -4 =$

5. $-2 + -10 =$

6. $12 + -15 =$

7. $-3 - -4 =$

8. $8 - -10 =$

9. $12 - 17 =$

10. $3 - -2 =$

✎ ✎ ✎ ✎ ✎

"C'mon," Noel called to the kids. "We've got to gno faster if we're to cnatch up with Mr. X. Hnere, at this ladder. Go dnown three rungs four times."

_____

You know that when someone says "times" what he is really doing is setting up a multiplication problem. Since Noel wants the kids to go down 3 rungs on the ladder 4 times, you can set it up this way:

$$-3 \times 4 =$$

Negative 3 because we're going down 3 rungs at a time. How many times? 4. Taylor got confused. He went 3 rungs –4 times. What happened to Taylor? He went –3 × 4 = ... so where does that put him?

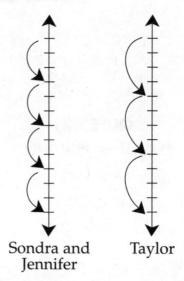

Sondra and
Jennifer
Taylor

Fortunately, it puts him on exactly the same spot as everyone else. He thought positive 3 rungs, which would mean going up, except that he had to do it a *negative* amount of times. So then he went backwards. –3 × 4 = –12. –4 × 3 = –12. The rule to remember in multiplication of a negative number is: When you multiply a negative number by a positive number, the result will always be negative.

What about a positive times a positive? That's easy. 2 × 2 = 4, just like always. A positive times a positive is positive. But, what about a negative times a negative? Think about it. (It's weird.) That means going in a negative direction a *negative* amount of times. In other words, the numbers are going backward. It's like saying "not . . . not," as in "I do not hate my homework *not*. The "nots" cancel out to say,"I do hate my homework!" It's the same with negative numbers. A negative times a negative cancels to a positive. The rule to remember: When you multiply a negative number by another negative number, the result will be a positive number. For instance, –3 × –5 = 15, regular old positive 15.

✎ ✎ ✎ ✎ ✎

"We're almost there," Noel called to the kids clinging to the ladder. "A fnew more ladders, couple more dank wet pnassage ways, and we'll gnet to X's chamber. From there you're non your own. If you can figure out X, you'll be all set. If not, you cnan't snay I didn't try."

"Thanks, Noel," The kids said.

"Think nothing of it. Now just go down that ladder one qnuarter of the way."

"Okay." The kids said. They were getting the hang of this negative stuff. The ladder had twelve rungs, so they went down three rungs.

Here's the problem the kids solved so easily. –12 divided by 4. So what if it has negative numbers, it is still a division problem. Just divide 12 by 4 and keep the negative sign. Just like in multiplication, in division if one number is positive and the other is negative, the answer is always negative.

What do you think happens when you divide a negative number by a negative number? How about –12 divided by –4? This yields a positive result, just like multiplying a negative by a negative. Math rules can seem a little crazy sometimes, but think of that as making them more exciting to learn.

✍ QUIZ #22 ✍
Multiplying and Dividing Negative Numbers

1. 3 × –4 =
2. –22 × –1=
3. –32 × –2 =
4. –3 × 0 =

5. $4 \times -5 =$

6. $-22 \div -1 =$

7. $35 \div -7 =$

8. $-24 \div 6 =$

9. $0 \div -2 =$

10. $-4 \div -2 =$

Now, if you're ready, you can try these next problems that combine everything you have learned so far. This stuff can get confusing; so whenever you see something (a hole, a plate of cookies . . .) you can't understand, try drawing a number line or some kind of visual picture to help yourself out. And, don't forget PEMDAS! The order of operations. Do parentheses first, then do out all the multiplication and division, then combine the positive and negative numbers you're left with.

✍ QUIZ #23 ◔
Review

1. $3 + -4(2 - 1) =$

2. $-5 - 7 + -2 =$

3. $-6 \div -3 \times -2 =$

4. $-1 + 1 + -1 + 1 =$

5. $-2(-3 + -4) - 17 =$

6. $-45 \div -9 + 7 =$

7. $-32 \times 5 \div 2 =$

8. $17 + 23 - -5(2 - 3) =$

9. $35 - 36 =$

10. $35 - -36 =$

Great job. Check the answers in the back of the book and read the explanations if you have any questions.

Chapter 10
Algebra

"Bye, Noel," the kids called out to the fat mole as it waddled away into the darkness. "Hey! Wait! Who is this Mr. X we're supposed to find? How will we know him when we see him?"

"Oh, him. Well, he's the mnost terrifying and inmpossible man on top of or underneath the earth," the mole said simply, as though it were no big deal at all. "Mr. X is the *unknown*. He can take on any shape, any face, any pnersonality. He's due any minute now, and frankly, I'd rather not run into him. He gives me the creeps. Bye, gotta go, see ya, toodle-oo."

The scratching, snuffling sounds of the mole faded slowly away. The kids could hear him clambering on to the nearest ladder, then he was gone.

"I *never* liked that freaky mole. Never," Taylor said.

"Oh, quit griping." Jennifer snapped. "We're still here, aren't we?"

"Yeah," said Taylor, "and we're farther away from the surface than ever."

"Sssssshhhhhh," said Sondra. "I hear something. Oh my God, I hear something! Here he comes. Quick! Hide!"

The kids tucked themselves away into the dark, wet, shadowy corners as best they could, and cowered. Even Jennifer was scared. They could hear something approaching. After a few moments, a dim figure appeared in the shadows of the tunnel, walking slowly and humming to itself. The figure was tall, thin, and stooped. Its feet scraped against the stone floor as it walked. As it got closer, the kids could hear that it hummed a very sad little tune.

"That couldn't be the terrifying Mr. *X*," Taylor whispered. "No one demented and cruel hums sad little tunes. Mr. *X* has eyes that glow like the fires of hell. And has long curved fangs dripping with poisonous saliva."

"No, it's a trick," Sondra said. "Mr. *X* is a shape-changer. He can look any way he wants to. Stay back."

"But he's the only one who can help us, even Noel the mole said so," Jennifer pleaded. "We've got to approach him. I'll do it." And before Sondra or Taylor could stop her, Jennifer was running down the tunnel toward Mr. *X*.

"Poor Jennifer," Taylor said, "she's doomed."

"Oh Taylor, I'm going to cry. This is so awful. What are we going to do?"

But after a few seconds they heard Jennifer saying, "C'mon you two, he's harmless, come and meet Mr. *X*."

Sondra went flying down the tunnel, happy to hear that her friend was okay. Taylor crept forward, still thinking there might be some trick awaiting him.

As it turned out, Mr. *X* was a harmless old man *without a face.* Mr. *X* had no face, just blank skin where his features should have been. When he talked a mouth suddenly appeared in the blankness, but as soon as he stopped the mouth just disappeared. His voice was oddly flat.

"It's true," Mr. *X* said in response to a question from Jennifer. "I can be anything I want to be."

"Well, why don't you make yourself something fantastic?" she asked.

"Well, I guess I have to *want* to do that first, and I don't want anything. I'm just plain old Mr. *X*. I don't even want a personality."

"Pretty terrifying, huh?" Jennifer said to Taylor.

"The terrifying part now is how is this guy supposed to help us?" Taylor said. "I'm sick of wandering around this place, *wherever* we are."

"Yeah, let's get out of here. Ask him how to get out of here," Sondra said. She didn't want to ask Mr. *X* herself because he did seem kind of creepy to her.

"How do we get out of here, Mr. X?" Jennifer asked simply.

"Gosh, I don't know," he said.

"You too, huh?" said Taylor. "Everybody's out to get us—*you too!*"

"Me, two? Okay," said the faceless Mr. X, and before their eyes, his face became a 2.

You see, X can be anything—any number. You've probably seen a math problem set up like this:

$$5 - x = 2$$

And it probably scared you. Did you think, "Geez, I've got enough trouble with just plain old numbers . . . if you start throwing letters in there I'll never get it"? Well, we've got news for you. *Mr. X is harmless.* All x means is some number—x is a **variable.** A variable is just a letter that stands in temporarily for a number that is unknown or changeable (it doesn't have to be x, by the way, x is only the most common letter used).

For example, a mathematician might say: Let $x = 2$. Okay.

If $x = 2$ then $x + 2$ equals 4

and $x + 7$ equals 9

and $x - 3$ equals -1

(Remember your negative numbers, they're important for algebra.)

How about $2x$? What does that mean? It means 2 times x. In algebra you need to get used to the idea that when numbers or variables are pressed together with nothing in between, it means to multiply. So if x equals 2, then $2x$ equals 4, because 2 times 2 is 4. When a variable has a number in front of it—$2x$, for example—the number in front is called the **coefficient.** In the example we just gave, 2 is the coefficient of x.

If $x = 2$ then $2x$ equals 4

and $3x$ equals 6

and $-7x$ equals -14 (that's just -7 times 2, of course it equals -14).

Another way to think of it is that $2x$ means you've got two x's ($x + x$), and $3x$ means you've got 3 x's ($x + x + x$). $-7x$ is seven $-x$'s ($-x - x - x - x - x - x - x$). Remember how addition and multiplication are related? Two times 3 is equal to $2 + 2 + 2$. The rules for math don't change because of the variables. $3x$ (which is x three times) is the same as $x + x + x$. So, to add $2x$ to $3x$ you just add the coefficients. $2x + 3x = 5x$. $3x - 6x = -3x$. Got it? Okay.

✍ QUIZ #24 ✍
Algebra

For questions 1 through 5, let $x = 3$.

1. $x + 1 =$ $3 + 1 = 4$
2. $x - 1 =$ $3 - 1 = 2$
3. $2x =$ $2(3) = 6$
4. $2(x) =$ $2(3) = 6$
5. $-x =$ -3

For 6 through 8, let $x = -2$.

6. $x - 2 =$ $3 - 2 = 1$
7. $-3x =$ $-3(3) = -9$
8. $4x - 6x =$ $4(3) - 6(3) = 12 - 18 = -6$

For 9 and 10, let $x = 12$.

9. $x + 9$ divided by $3 =$
10. $2x - (x + 3) =$

$2(12) - (12 + 3) =$ ✏ ✏ ✏ ✏

"*Weird!*" Taylor cried as he stared at the number Mr. X's face had become. "This guy is truly freaky."

$2(12) - (12 + 3)$

$24 - 15 = 9$

"Yes, I am a bit strange, I admit," Mr. X said, "but not someone to be frightened of, I hope. I can change into any number at all. A harmless talent."

"But that doesn't help us because we don't know how to get out of here. We don't know exactly what we want," Jennifer said sadly.

"Oh! Why didn't you say so in the first place? That's my specialty!" Mr. X said. "That's my favorite task of all. I can be the *Unknown*."

This is where Mr. X really comes into his own. (He is a he, isn't he? Maybe a she? Or both? Okay, X is a little weird.) When you don't know exactly what you're looking for, x comes in really handy.

The key to using x is the equal sign. You're used to seeing math problems like this:

2 + 3 = ? 5

6 divided by 2 = ? 12

56 × 2 = ? 102

Because you're used to seeing equal signs with nothing after them—equal signs just hanging out waiting for an answer—it's easy to think that an equal sign is some kind of strange mathematical question mark. It *isn't*. An equal sign means you're looking at an **equation.** An equation means the numbers on either side of the equals sign are perfectly balanced. Get used to thinking of an equal sign as a balance, like this:

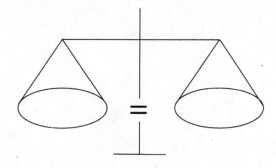

When you are doing algebra—working with variables—
always think of an equation as a balance. If you do, you'll
be able to solve problems like this:

$$x = 4 - 3$$

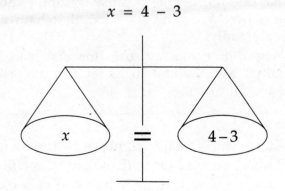

So $x = 1$, or

$$1 = 4 - 3 \text{ or}$$

$$1 = 1$$

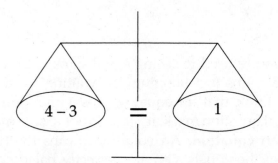

So the rest is easy: they all balance. They're all the same.

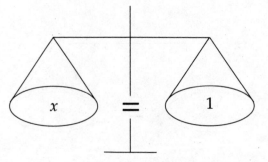

Now try this one.

$$x + 3 = 4$$

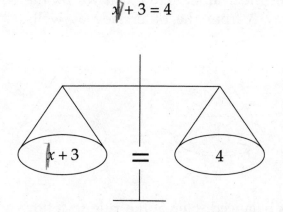

At the moment, x is unknown. We want to solve for the unknown, also known as solving for the variable. All that these expressions mean is that you are trying to figure out what number x is. The way to figure this out is by **isolating the variable.** That means getting the letter (we're using x) all alone on one side of the equation, and all the regular numbers on the other side. How? Like this:

$$x + 3 = 4$$
$$- 3$$

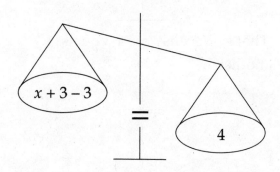

Now the equation isn't equal; it's messed up. We took away the 3 to get the x alone. How can we fix the equation? By taking away 3 from the other side as well:

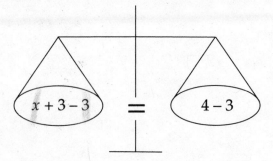

$$x + 3 - 3 = 4 - 3$$

Now it's balanced. Here's the rule to follow when you're doing algebra: Whatever you do to one side of the equation you must do to the other side.

Here's what the problem we tried looks like now.

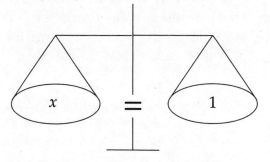

$$x = 1$$

That's it. That's the answer: x equals 1.

Let's try another.

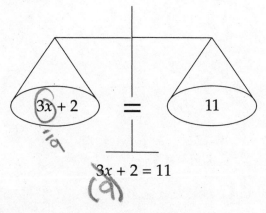

$$3x + 2 = 11$$

What do we do? Isolate the variable. How? By always doing the same thing to both sides. It can get tricky so follow us: First subtract 2 from each side.

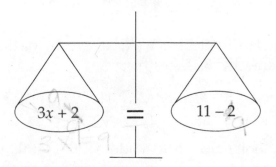

Okay, what's left?

$3x = 9$ Now what do we do? Well, it's simple. Because x is multiplied by 3, we need to undo that. We need to know what just one x is, so we divide $3x$ by 3. Let's write it out the long way.

$$3 \cdot x \div 3$$

Another way to look at it is:

$$\frac{3 \cdot x}{3}$$

Cancel the threes. What do you get? x! By itself! But we'd better not forget to divide the other side. Nine divided by 3 is 3. Here's what our equation looks like now. *Voila!*

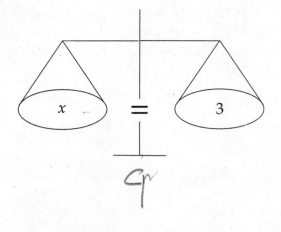

$x = 3$. Great! But did you know we could have easily gone wrong? Take a look. What if we'd decided to divide by 3 first, and then subtract the 2?

$$3x + 2 = 11$$

If we'd tried to divide first, we'd have to divide the equation's entire left side by 3. Like this:

$$\frac{(3x+2)}{3} = \frac{11}{3}$$

Does that look harder? It should—it is. Not that it's illegal. You won't get the wrong answer working this way. You'd just get frustrated. There's an order to follow in solving an algebra problem and it's quite simple.

First, combine everything that can be combined.

Second, do all the addition and/or subtraction.

Third, do the division, *then* the multiplication.

Let's try a problem that needs the first and second guidelines and some of the third. (We'll look at rule three more carefully in another example.)

$$2x + 3 - 3x + 5 = 17$$

First, combine. You can't combine $2x$ and 3; you can't combine $-3x$ and 5! *Never try to combine (add or subtract) a normal number and a variable.* In this problem you should combine $2x$ and $-3x$. What is $2x - 3x$? Right—it equals $-x$. (You don't have to write $-1x$. -1 is understood to be the coefficient. Just as 1 is understood to be the coefficient of x.) Now combine 3 and 5. That's easy. 8. Okay, let's look at what we've got.

$$-x + 8 = 17$$

Subtract 8 from both sides.

$$-x + 8 = 17$$
$$\quad -8 \quad -8$$
$$\quad\quad = \;\; 9$$

$-x = 9$. Are you done? Nope. How do we get rid of that pesky negative sign? Easy. Remember that $-x$ means $-1x$. Just like before, you divide by -1. What's $-1x$ divided by -1? A negative divided by a negative is a positive. One divided by 1 is 1.

$$\frac{-x}{-1} = x$$

Remember to do the same thing to both sides. Nine divided by -1. Okay, same rules. A positive divided by a negative equals a negative. *Always.* Nine divided by 1 is 9, so the answer is -9. Did you notice what happens when you divide by -1? All that changes is the sign, which flips: a positive becomes a negative, a negative becomes a positive. Here's what our problem looks like now:

$$x = -9$$

Are we finished? Yep.

Let's do one more.

$$\frac{3x}{2} + 2 = 17$$

First, is there anything to combine? Nope. Okay, step two, is there anything to add or subtract? You bet—2. Subtract 2 from both sides.

$$\frac{3x}{2} + \frac{2}{} = \frac{17}{-2}$$

$$\frac{-2}{\dfrac{3x}{2}} = 15$$

Now, $3x$ divided by 2. How on earth do we undo that? Simple! The x is being divided by 2, so now, *multiply* both sides by 2.

$$\cancel{2} \cdot \frac{3x}{\cancel{2}} = 15 \cdot 2$$

$$3x = 30$$

You can take it from here, right? Divide both sides by 3.

$$x = 10$$

✍ QUIZ #25 ✍
Review

1. $x + 3 = 7$
2. $x - 9 = 1$
3. $3x = 12$
4. $-3x = -12$
5. $x + 2 + x = 4$
6. $3x + 7 - x = 13$
7. $\dfrac{3x}{2} = 18$
8. $\dfrac{20}{x} = 10$
9. $\dfrac{7}{2x} + 4 = 18$
10. $\dfrac{9x}{3} + \dfrac{2x}{3} = 11$

✏ ✏ ✏ ✏ ✏

"Wait a minute, you can be the *Unknown*?" Sondra asked Mr. X.

"Oh yes, I'm quite good at it."

"Well," said Sondra, "we don't know how to get out of here. That's the unknown for us."

"Yes," said Mr. *X* in his flavorless, empty voice.

"So be the unknown for us . . . be the way out of here."

"Oh, sure, why didn't you say so in the first place?" Mr. *X* began to stroll off down the winding tunnels. "You realize I don't have the foggiest idea where I'm going."

"No problem, *X*. Just walk," the kids said, following at Mr. *X*'s heels.

After a few minutes of wandering in what seemed like aimless circles through the dark, Mr. *X* said, "Oh, look, well, what do you know? Here we are."

High above the kids could see a small, bright circle of light. As they walked and climbed and crawled slowly upward, it grew wider.

"Has anyone noticed that for the past five minutes we've been walking on the edge of a cliff?" Jennifer asked.

The other kids froze in their tracks and looked to the side. Jennifer was right. The ground fell away in a sheer drop inches from where they walked. It was too dark to see the bottom. But you could just *feel* that it was a long, long way down.

"I forgot about the cliff, silly me," Mr. *X* said in a stupid sort of way.

"Just how d-deep is that chasm?" Taylor twitched.

"Deep? Why, it has no final depth," Mr. *X* replied. "It just plunges down forever into negative infinity."

"That's it. I'm jumping. I can't take it any more. I'll just fall. Fall and fall forever. Good-bye, cruel world," Taylor cried. He stood, frozen, at the edge of the cliff. "What? Isn't anybody going to stop me? Nice friends I've got."

"Just consider yourself lucky I don't push you," Jennifer snapped at him.

The kids trooped on toward the circle of light. They could hear the familiar sounds of the outside world. The scent of green grass wafted into the tunnel.

"Good-bye, Mr. *X*. Thanks for everything. And if you see Noel the Negativity Mole, tell him 'hi' from us."

"Alright. Bye, kids. Glad I could be of help."

Jennifer was the first one to crawl out of the hole. She helped Sondra out and then Taylor. They stood blinking in the late afternoon light. It was the good old familiar world. It was all so familiar. It was extremely familiar. It was much, much too familiar.

"Hey, we're back at the oak tree!" They all shouted at once.

Sure enough, the tunnel exited right there at the oak tree.

"Great, we're right back where we started," Sondra said, "Now all we need is Beauregard to show up. Hey! Poor Beauregard! He must be worried, terribly worried. We'd better find him and tell him we're okay. For all he knows we could be dead."

"That's very thoughtful of you, Sondra," said Beauregard's silky, sleepy voice from high above in the tree.

The kids looked up, and there was Beauregard, yawning and stretching up in his favorite nook. "Yes, oh heavens yes, I was *terribly* worried. *Especially* when you didn't recognize me in that *ridiculous* Noel the Mole costume, with that *ridiculous* voice. Heavens, I was worried you'd all completely lost your minds." And with that, Beauregard stretched, yawned one last time, and went back to sleep.

Review Appendix

WHOLE NUMBERS

This section is designed to help you brush up on addition, subtraction, multiplication, and division with whole numbers.

So what are whole numbers? Whole numbers have no fractions or decimals and are not negative. Whole numbers are what you probably think of as "normal" numbers.

As long as we're on the subject of terminology (*terminology* is a fancy word for "the names of things"), here's a checklist of terms you should already know, but that are covered in this review:

borrowing	factors	product
carrying	multiply	quotient
digits	odd	remainder
division	parentheses	sum
even	primes	times

If any of these words are unfamiliar to you, look for the **boldface** of that term. For example, if you don't know what a "sum" is, look for **sum.** You'll find it on page 185.

ADDITION

Here's an addition problem: What is twelve plus seven? How would you write it out?

$$12 + 7 = ?$$

There's another way to write it too.

$$\begin{array}{r} 12 \\ +\ \underline{7} \\ 19 \end{array}$$

Especially when you use bigger numbers, you'll find it helpful to stack them like we just did. How come? Well, to talk about that we need to talk a little bit more about numbers themselves.

Look at what we call the **digit places** of a number. A **digit** is one of the group of numbers 0 through 9. A one-digit number, such as 5, is a number that only has, you guessed it, one digit. A two-digit number has two digits. Examples are 23 or 15. These numbers are made up of two digits. How about 13? That's right, a two-digit number. How about 22? That's right, a two-digit number.

The places of the digits matter. In the number 13, the 3 is in the **ones** or **units digit** place (either ones or units is okay). The 1 is in the **tens digit** place.

That means the number 13 is made up of three 1s and one 10.

$$1 + 1 + 1 + 10 = 13$$

Bigger numbers work this way too. Think of 145. The ones digit is 5, the tens digit is 4, and the **hundreds digit** is 1. So, 145 is made up of five ones (5), four tens (40), and one one-hundred (100).

When you stack numbers up to add them, you line them up by their digits places to make sure that you add the ones place to the ones place, the tens place to the tens place, and so on.

Suppose you had to add 19 to 13? Well, first you want to stack the numbers, lining them up by their digit places.

$$19$$
$$\underline{+13}$$

First add the 9 and the 3 in the ones place. What happens? You get 12; just look on the number line.

Now think about 12 for a second. It has a 2 in the ones place, and a 1 in the tens place. That's how you will add it. Put the 2 in the ones place of your **sum**, and add the 1 to the tens place of the other tens. (By the way, a sum is the answer to an addition problem.)

$$\overset{1}{}$$
$$19$$
$$\underline{+13}$$
$$32$$

You now have three ones in the tens place. So put a 3 in the tens place of your number.

$$19 + 13 = 32$$

Of course you can add with the number line as well, but this method of moving the numbers to the next digits place, called **carrying** by mathematicians, will be the easier method to use as the numbers get bigger. Try to imagine adding 199 to 73 using the number line. What a pain!

If you think you can handle the **carrying**, try this problem:

What is 100 + 125 + 95 + 75 + 75?

It's an addition problem. The best way to handle any math problem is to write it on paper, and the best way to handle an addition problem is to stack the numbers up.

$$\begin{array}{r} 100 \\ 125 \\ 95 \\ 75 \\ +75 \end{array}$$

How much is that? To find out, line up the numbers by their digit places, just as you did before. Then, add up each digit place and carry the numbers again.

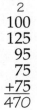

Did you get the same answer? If not, check your work. Did the units digit place add up to 20, so you left a 0 and carried the 2? Did the tens place add up to 27, so you left the 7 and carried the 2? Did the hundreds place add up to 4? Always be careful to check your work. Checking takes time, but getting the right answer is worth it.

Hey, what about adding the numbers in a different order? For instance 100 + 95 + 75 + 125 + 75 = 470. Does it make any difference? Nope. Adding the numbers in a different order doesn't make any difference in your answer. No matter how you group the numbers in an addition problem, they will always give the same sum.

95 + 100 + 125 + 75 + 75 = 470

This principle has an important sounding name. It's called the **Associative Law of Addition**. Knowing that name never helped anyone to get a math problem right. Knowing the *idea* though—knowing that when a bunch of numbers are added together, those numbers can be grouped however you want them to be—can make many problems easier. Suppose you had to add:

$$3 + 9 + 7 + 6 + 4 + 5 + 1 + 5 = \,?$$

You could add them in the order given, one at a time, and you'd get the right answer. But a better way would be to group together numbers that add up to 10.

$$
\begin{array}{cccc}
3 & 9 & 6 & 5 \\
+7 & +1 & +4 & +5 \\
\hline
10 & 10 & 10 & 10
\end{array}
$$

Now count up the tens. Four tens. Forty. Pretty easy, huh?

Here's the "official" way you would write out that grouping.

$$(7 + 3) + (9 + 1) + (6 + 4) + (5 + 5) = 40$$

By the way, those **parentheses ( )** surrounding the numbers tell you which part of the math problem should be done first. Because this problem is *all* addition, the paretheses don't matter, but if some of the operations were multiplication or division, the paretheses would be very important. Chapter 2 gives into that idea in detail. You'll be seeing a lot more parentheses later.

✍ QUIZ A ✍
Addition Review

1. 15 + 29 =
2. 111 + 23 =
3. 219 + 393 =
4. 313 + 32 + 54 =
5. 4,113 + 332 + 19 + 193 =

6. Sondra's cat had thirteen kittens, and Taylor's cat had twenty-two kittens. How many kittens do they have altogether?

7. Taylor has twenty-eight race cars and Jennifer has one hundred and thirteen race cars. How many cars do they have altogether?

8. In the first month of school last year, Sondra missed two days. In the third month of school, Sondra missed seventeen days (she had her appendix taken out). In the last month of school, Sondra missed nine days. If Sondra missed no other days of school last year, how many days did she miss in total?

9. Taylor has a stamp collection with only Canadian, English, and Australian stamps. If he has thirty-two Canadian stamps, forty-nine English stamps, and sixty-seven Australian stamps, how many stamps does he have altogether in his collection?

10. All the kids went to the seashore this summer. Rose brought back twelve shells, Lionel brought back thirty-one shells, Sondra brought back seventeen shells, Taylor brought back two hundred and sixty-three shells, and Jennifer didn't bring back any shells because she was busy riding the waves. How many shells did they bring back altogether?

SUBTRACTION

Subtraction can be thought of as the opposite of addition. In addition, you learned about carrying. To do subtraction, you'll need to know about something called **borrowing.** In the same way that subtraction is the opposite of addition, borrowing is the opposite of carrying.

Take a look at this problem:

$$24 - 5$$

Twenty-four is larger than 5, but to figure out the digits place you need to subtract 5 from 4. How? Well, if you didn't have enough flour to bake a loaf of bread you might **borrow** some from your next-door neighbor. Numbers do the same thing. They borrow from their neighbor. In the problem 24 – 5, the 4 "borrows" from the tens place. Now subtract 5 from 14 instead of from 4, and you will still have a 1 left in the tens place.

$$\begin{array}{r} {}^{1}2\!\!\!/4 \\ -\ 5 \\ \hline 19 \end{array}$$

A short cut you can use to make subtraction easier is to subtract numbers in parts. For example the number 5 can be thought of as (4 + 1). So instead of 24 – 5, the question can also be thought of as 24 – 4, which is 20, then 20 – 1, which is 19. This is especially useful when you need to subtract numbers in your head. You can also borrow with bigger numbers. How about 101 – 37?

$$101 - 37$$

Well, 1 minus 7 doesn't work, so you borrow from the tens place. Since there is only a 0 there, you have to look more to the hundreds place. Instead of a 0 in the tens place, look at it as a 10. You borrow a 1, leaving 9, so you have 11 – 7.

$$\begin{array}{r} {}^{0}1\!\!\!/\,{}^{9}0\!\!\!/1 \\ -\ 37 \end{array}$$

Well, 11 – 7 is 4, and 9 – 3 ?

$$\begin{array}{r} {}^{0}1\!\!\!/\,{}^{9}0\!\!\!/1 \\ -\ 37 \\ \hline 64 \end{array}$$

Here's another kind of problem. Let's say we have 2 cookies and you have 19. You have how many more cookies than we do? The way to figure out this question is by subtraction. Whenever you want to know *how much more* someone has, subtract. It is easiest to write this question:

$$19 - 2 =$$

Well? 19 – 2 = 17, so you have 17 more cookies than we do. A way to check your subtraction is with addition. (Remember, subtraction is the opposite of addition.) Is 2 + 17 = 19? It is.

What about a problem like this: You start with 12 cookies, but then you eat 2 and give away 3 to friends. How many would you have left? The easiest thing to do is to subtract numbers one at a time. For example:

$$12 \text{ cookies} - 2 \text{ cookies} = 10$$

Then

$$10 \text{ cookies} - 3 \text{ cookies} = 7$$

Don't stack up more than two numbers in a subtraction problem. But, no matter what, you can always go to the number line if you run into trouble.

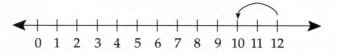

Sometimes subtracting gets a little long for the number line, though. Then you may have to use some other techniques.

Subtraction Review

1. 27 − 12 =

2. 57 − 24 =

3. 131 − 19 =

4. 134 − 29 =

5. 1001 − 107 =

6. Jennifer has thirty-nine tissues. If she gives twenty-five of them to Taylor, how many does she have left?

7. Taylor took twenty-three hamburgers to the barbecue, ate some of them, but then had to take twelve back without eating them because he overestimated his appetite. How many hamburgers did Taylor eat?

8. Taylor has two hundred and twenty-five marbles, and Sondra has one hundred and thirty-two marbles. How many more marbles does Taylor have than Sondra?

9. Taylor had one hundred and seventeen plastic planes. If thirty-nine of them melted in the sun, how many did he have left?

10. Jennifer has read one thousand and twelve books. If forty of these are science books and one hundred of them are detective novels, how many of them are neither science books nor detective novels?

MULTIPLICATION

Multiplication is related to addition. Suppose you had to add five numbers. If the five numbers were all different, you'd have no choice but to add them. But if you had to add the same number five times in a row, then there's a shorter way, called multiplication.

Let's take 3 + 3 + 3 + 3 + 3. We're adding the same number—3—a bunch of times in a row. So instead of adding, we can **multiply**. Multiplication is used to make life a little bit easier.

Instead of adding the 3 five times, you say, "three multiplied by five." Another way to say the same thing is to say, "three **times** five." That makes sense, doesn't it? Because you are adding the 3 five *times*. Multiplication can look like any of these:

$$3 \times 5$$

$$3 \bullet 5$$

$$(3)(5)$$

$$3(5)$$

Of course, the result of 3×5 is the same as that of $3 + 3 + 3 + 3 + 3$. Both of these operations equal 15. Some cool things about multiplication are:

Any number times 0 is equal to 0. So, $23 \times 0 = 0$. $5{,}173{,}294{,}756{,}210 \times 0 = 0$

any number times 1 is equal to itself. So, $15 \times 1 = 15$. $2 \times 1 = 2$. $16{,}000{,}000{,}000 \times 1 = 16{,}000{,}000{,}000$.

When you add, the final result is called the **sum**. So, $3 + 3 + 3 + 3 + 3$ gives a sum of 15. When you multiply, the final result is called the **product**. So, 3×5 gives a product of 15.

Let's try another multiplication problem. Suppose you have five friends and you want to give each of them four presents (because you're generous and kind, or else because you're going to ask them later to do you a really big favor). This problem could be set up as $4 + 4 + 4 + 4 + 4$, but at this point we hope you'd say to yourself, "Let's see, that's four presents five times," then set it up as 4×5. Excellent: $4 \times 5 = 20$.

An interesting thing about multiplication is that it works in both directions. For instance, you could have said, "Let's see, that's five friends four times" ... $5 \times 4 = 20$ (which is the same as saying $5 + 5 + 5 + 5$).

Being able to switch the order of the numbers is called the **Commutative Law of Multiplication**. It's like the Associative Law, but with multiplication instead. Here is an easy way to see this. Here are 20 friends:

Circle them in groups. You can make four groups of five friends each, right?

Now here is the same diagram. Try to circle five groups of four friends each. That's easy too, right?

That's how the Commutative Law of Multiplication works.

Multiplication will make many of your calculations much faster and easier, but you have some work to do first. You have to memorize the multiplication tables. That way the instant someone says, "What is 4 × 5?" you will know the answer is 20.

Times Table

×	2	3	4	5	6	7	8	9	10	11	12
2	4	6	8	10	12	14	16	18	20	22	24
3	6	9	12	15	18	21	24	27	30	22	36
4	8	12	16	20	24	28	32	36	40	44	48
5	10	15	20	25	30	35	40	45	50	55	60
6	12	18	24	30	36	42	48	54	60	66	72
7	14	21	28	35	42	49	56	63	70	77	84
8	16	24	32	40	48	56	64	72	80	88	96
9	18	27	36	45	54	63	72	81	90	99	108
10	20	30	40	50	60	70	80	90	100	110	120
11	22	33	44	55	66	77	88	99	110	121	132
12	24	36	48	60	72	84	96	108	120	132	144

Whenever you get a chance, study your times tables. Soon you won't even have to look, you'll know them all. There are some wonderful things about the times tables. For instance, look at the nines column. All of the numbers in this column are mirrors of each other, 09 and 90, 18 and 81, 27 and 72. Amazing, right? All those numbers are 9 times something: 9 times 2, 9 times 3, and so on. These numbers— 8, 18, 27, and so on—are all **multiples** of 9. Multiples are all the possible products of a number. Now look at the fives column of the times table. Here's something to notice: all the multiples of 5 on the times table end in 5 or 0. That's because *all* multiples of 5 end in 5 or 0. Even 5 times one billion and three must end in a 5 or a 0. (By looking at the times table can you guess which one it ends in? It ends in a 5 just like 5 × 3 does.) Think about this too: a great trick when you are multiplying a number by 10 is to put a zero at the end of the number you are multiplying. This short cut works because whenever you multiply by 10, you're adding a whole set of 10, so you just add another digit place. So, 10 × 4 = 40. What is 10 × 5? Just add a zero. It's 50.

How about to multiply by 100? Any guesses? To multiply by 100, put two zeroes at the end of the number. So, 4 × 100 = 400. How about 5 × 100? That's right, 500.

You might even take a guess about how many zeroes you add when you multiply by 1,000. Well, how many zeroes after the 1? That's right, three. So that's how many zeroes you add. And it keeps working like this with all multiples of 10. And if you multiply by 1? Well, if you have one box of five cookies, how many cookies?

$$1 \times 5 = 5$$

One times any number is that number.

Here's another term that you should know: **factors.** Whole numbers that multiply to form a product are called factors. For example 5 × 2 is 10, so 5 and 2 are factors of 10. One and 10 also multiply to form 10, so 1 and 10 are also factors of 10.

Do any other whole numbers multiply to form 10? (Remember, just whole numbers, we're not counting fractions for any smarty-pants out there.) No. So 10 has only four factors, 1 and 10, and 2 and 5.

How about 12? What are the factors of 12? Well first you start with 1 and 12 When listing factors of a number, it is best to start with 1 and the number itself, then go to the number's next factor that is larger than 1. So, 1 and 12, 2 and 6, and 3 and 4. The number 12 has six factors: 1, 2, 3, 4, 6, 12.

How about the number 13? Well, first you have 1 and 13. Then what? Look at your times table, do any numbers there multiply to form 13? Nope, that's because 13 has only two factors, 1 and itself. A number with only two factors is called a **prime number**. Mathematicians think prime numbers are cool, and they love to multiply and combine them in strange ways to see what kinds of patterns emerge. Is 6 a prime number? Nope, because it has 1 and 6, and 2, and 3 as factors. Is five a prime number? Yup, because its only factors are 1 and 5. Is 2 a prime number? Yes, its only factors are 1 and itself. In fact, 2 is the only *even* prime number. Is 1 a prime number? Actually, this may surprise you. No, 1 is not a prime number. Why? Because 1 has so many unique characteristics that mathematicians think it belongs in a class all by itself. Mathematicians say that 1 is *special*.

Now that you know how to multiply the smaller numbers in the times tables, you will find that to multiply larger numbers is similar, and quite simple. It just takes a little more time because there are more numbers involved. You multiply larger numbers one digits place at a time.

Let's start with 5 × 20. 5 × 0 equals 0, so write down 0. Now do 5 × 2. That equals 10. Write down 10 on the other side of 0. That's the answer—100.

You see, even though 5 × 0 is nothing, it's important to write down the 0 because it occupies the units place; that way when you multiply 5 × 2 you put the answer in the right place. If you had forgotten to put down the 0, you'd have gotten 5 × 20 equals ten, and that is definitely wrong. The only hard part in multiplying (once you know your times tables) is keeping the places straight.

$$\text{Let's try} \quad \begin{array}{r} 23 \\ \times\ 5 \\ \hline \end{array}$$

First multiply 5 × 3. That equals 15. Now multiply 5 × 2 but don't forget that the 2 is in the tens place, so it isn't really 2 at all but 20. 5 × 2 is 10, but 5 times a 2 in the tens place is 10 with another 0 dropped down. That equals 100. Add 15 to 100. The answer is 115. (If you write out a string of 23 fives and add them all up you should get 115. We don't recommend you do that though because it would be really dull.)

How about 5 × 123? That's 5 × 3 = 15; 5 × 20 = 100; and 5 × 100, which is the same as five times 1 with two 0s dropped down, which is 500. Now add 500 + 100 + 15. The answer is 615.

There's an even faster way to do all this. It's the way most people do most multiplication and it's a way you should learn to do too. Instead of breaking a number like 123 into 100, 20, and 3 to multiply by five in three very separate steps, we can compress the whole multiplication operation a little by "carrying" and do 5 x 123 all in one step without any addition. It's very much like the carrying we did in addition. Let's try 123 × 5 again.

$$\begin{array}{r} 123 \\ \times\ 5 \\ \hline \end{array}$$

We start, just as before, with 5 × 3. The answer is still 15, but this time we only write down the number on the right, 5, and we carry the number on the left, 1.

$$\begin{array}{r} {}^{1}\ \ \\ 123 \\ \times 5 \\ \hline 5 \end{array}$$

Now we multiply just like before, 5 × 2; the answer is 10. Now add the number you carried, 10 + 1 is 11. Just like before, write down the number on the right, 1, and carry the number on the left, 1.

$$\begin{array}{r} {}^{1\,1}\ \\ 123 \\ \times 5 \\ \hline 15 \end{array}$$

Now, multiply 5 × 1, that equals 5, and add the number you carried, 1. 5 + 1 is 6.

$$\begin{array}{r} {}^{1\,1}\ \\ 123 \\ \times 5 \\ \hline 615 \end{array}$$

Phew! Okay, one more.

$$\begin{array}{r} 23 \\ \times\, 15 \\ \hline \end{array}$$

First do 5 × 3 = 15. Write down the 5, carry the 1. Now do 5 × 2 = 10 . . . and don't forget to add the 1 that you carried.

$$\begin{array}{r} ^{1} \\ 23 \\ \times\, 15 \\ \hline 115 \end{array}$$

Now it's time to multiply by the 1 in 15. The first thing you do is count how many places over you are. The 1 is one place over, so drop down a 0 to hold that place.

$$\begin{array}{r} ^{1} \\ 23 \\ \times\, 15 \\ \hline 115 \\ 0 \end{array}$$

Now you just multiply 1 × 3, 3 and 1 × 2, 2 and write those down.

$$\begin{array}{r} 23 \\ \times\, 15 \\ \hline 115 \\ +\, 230 \\ \hline \end{array}$$

Add it all up.

$$\begin{array}{r} ^{1} \\ 23 \\ \times\, 15 \\ \hline 115 \\ +\, 230 \\ \hline 345 \end{array}$$

Pay attention to how those digits are lined up, and you'll never have any trouble with multiplication.

Let's look a little bit more at why this works as it does. Why do you move that second number to the left? Well, you are multiplying by a 1 that is in the tens place, so you move your whole product over to the tens place. When we multiplied 15 times 23 we actually broke 15 down into 5 + 10 to get our answer. First we multiplied by 5 then, by dropping down that 0, we multiplied by 10. Then we put the pieces back together again when we added. This is one illustration of an important rule called the **Distributive Law**.

It looks like this: a (b + c) = ab + ac.

If that looks like the craziest math you ever saw, don't sweat it, because it looks much harder than it is. The letters each stand for a number. Mathematicians use letters to say you could put *any number* in place of that letter. The distributive law is important, and here's what you should know about it for now: If you can multiply 15 × 23 then you are already using distribution without even being aware of it. So when it comes time to learn distribution it should be a snap; you already know it.

✍ QUIZ C ✍
Multiplication Review

1. 3 × 14 =

2. 4 × 10 =

3. 14 × 10 =

4. 23 × 14 =

5. 5 × 2 =

6. Jennifer has two groups of five books each. How many books does she have?

7. Taylor has ten bottles of jelly beans, and each bottle contains exactly seven jelly beans (not the best deal). How many jelly beans does Taylor in have total?

8. Sondra has ten bags, and inside each bag are ten spiders. (She's about to play a mean trick on somebody.) How many spiders does Sondra have in total?

9. Taylor has twenty-two separate boxes, and inside each box are exactly thirty-three cars. How many race cars does Taylor have? And before you even do the problem, do you think he has more than one thousand or fewer than one thousand?

10. Jennifer has been collecting centipede legs for a long time. In her bedroom she has exactly one hundred and three jars, each filled with forty-three legs (yuck). How many centipede legs are in her collection? And before you do the problem, do you think she has more or fewer than five hundred legs? More or fewer than one thousand legs?

DIVISION

Division helps you figure out how to break up numbers into smaller parts of equal size. Division isn't very complicated; it's just the opposite of multiplication. Remember back on page 193 when you circled numbers of friends? We decided to look at that problem as a multiplication problem. We might very well have looked at it as a division problem and said, "Well, if I've got twenty presents, how can I divide them evenly among five friends?" How would we answer this question? We have twenty presents, and we want to divide them into five groups, one group for each friend. You would make five groups of four presents each.

Everyone has an equal number of presents. From your multiplication table you know 5 × 4 = 20, so, 20 ÷ 5 = 4. And there's another good reason to know your times table. Because division is the reverse of multiplication, we could just as easily call the times table the division table.

There are a few ways you will see the division operation written out in math. "Twenty divided by five" can look like any of these:

$$20 \div 5$$

$$
\begin{array}{r}
5\overline{)20} \\
\underline{20} \\
5
\end{array}
$$

$$20/5$$

No matter how it looks, division is the opposite of multiplication.

A number is always **divisible** by its factors. (Remember factors from page 195?) Divisible means the number can be evenly divided by, with none left over. How does this work? Well, any number divided by 1 is itself. What is 20 ÷ 1? It's 20.

How about 9,999,999 ÷ 1? That's 9,999,999. (By the way, how do you say that number? Nine million nine hundred ninety-nine thousand nine hundred and ninety-nine. Whew.)

Okay, let's say you're dividing up those presents again, and this time you've decided to give presents to just two of your friends because the other three acted like jerks the last time you saw them. Now you've got twenty presents to divide between just two friends. Here's what the problem would look like:

$$2\overline{)20}$$

Usually when you divide a two-digit number, you go one digit at a time starting at the left. Does 2 go into 2? Sure it does. How many groups of 2 are there in 2? Only one group. That's because any number divided by itself is equal to 1. So you put a 1 on top, exactly above the 2.

$$
\begin{array}{r}
1 \\
2\overline{)20}
\end{array}
$$

Now, the next digit. How many groups of 2 are there in 0? There are none, no groups of 2 in 0. So you write a 0 above this place. That's because 0 divided by any number is equal to 0.

$$\frac{10}{2\,\overline{)\,20\,}}$$

Each friend would get ten presents. That means you can divide the presents down the middle into two equal halves. There is another way to say this in math language: Any number that can be divided into two equal groups is called **even**. In other words, if you can divide a number by two without any left over, that number is even. If you can't divide a number by two, that number is called **odd**.

Do you think 0 is even? Try it out: Two people want to share zero cookies evenly. How many will each person get? 0. Will there be any left over? Nope, so 0 is divisible by 2; 0 is even. Can you divide three cookies evenly between two people? (And no breaking cookies, we're talking about whole cookies here.) No, there will always be one left over, so 3 is not even, 3 is odd.

THINK ABOUT THIS

You can never divide any number by 0. Why? Just because. You think we're kidding, right? You think there's some answer that we're holding back because you aren't old enough to understand? Well honest, we aren't. You just can't. It's weird, but in standard mathematics—the kind mathematicians used to design computers, or to calculate where a planet will be a million years from now, or to figure out the speed of light, or to weigh a single atom—division by 0 isn't allowed. To be fair, mathematicians don't exactly say, "You can't," they say, "Division by 0 is *undefined*." What that means is, "Okay, maybe it's possible somehow; but we haven't agreed on exactly how to do it, *so don't try it Buster*." Dividing by 0 makes mathematicians nervous. And we still say it's weird.

Okay, here's a question: You've got 120 presents; can you divide them evenly among five friends, and if you can, how many presents does each friend get? To answer the first part of this question ask yourself whether 120 is divisible by 5. What do you think? Do you remember about the fives column? Look back to your times tables. All of the numbers in the fives columns ended in 5 or 0. The truth is, any number ending in 5 or 0, no matter how big or how small, is divisible by 5. So what about 120? Yes, it's definitely divisible by 5.

Next, set up your division problem. You want to divide 120 into five groups, one for each kid, so 120 is what is being divided—it goes under the roof.

$$5 \overline{)120}$$

Start with the left-most number. How many 5s are there in 1? None, so you need to move to the right and try with a bigger number. Instead of just the left-most number, you combine it with the one next to it.

$$5 \overline{)120}$$

How many 5s are there in 12? There are two 5s in 12. Write 2 above the 12.

You are probably saying to yourself, but two 5s makes 10, not 12—what do I do with the difference? Well, you're on the right track. Two 5s do make 10; to check your work and make the problem easier, you are going to write that 10 down below the 12.

$$\begin{array}{r} 2 \\ 5 \overline{)120} \\ 10 \\ \hline \end{array}$$

Now, subtract the 10 from the 12 to see how many you have left over.

$$\begin{array}{r} 2 \\ 5 \overline{)120} \\ 10 \\ \hline 2 \end{array}$$

You still have that 0 on the end. To finish off this division problem, drop that last digit down to join your leftover 2.

$$
\begin{array}{r}
24 \\
5{\overline{\smash{\big)}\,120}} \\
\underline{10} \\
20
\end{array}
$$

How many 5s are there in 20? There are four. Write that down above that last digit, and you are done.

$$
\begin{array}{r}
24 \\
5{\overline{\smash{\big)}\,120}} \\
\underline{10} \\
20
\end{array}
$$

You can check your work now, by multiplying what is on top by what is on the outside. That means, multiply 24 by 5.

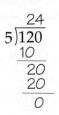

$$
\begin{array}{r}
24 \\
5{\overline{\smash{\big)}\,120}} \\
\underline{10} \\
20 \\
\underline{20} \\
0
\end{array}
$$

Does it give you 120? It sure does. The great thing is, this will work on any division problem. Always check your work this way, and you can be sure to get more problems right.

ANOTHER THING TO THINK ABOUT

To check if an integer is divisible by 2 (or even, in other words), look at its units digit. If the units digit is even, then the whole number is even.

Sometimes (quite often, in fact) something you want to divide doesn't divide up perfectly even. Suppose you had ten cookies to divide among three friends. Each friend would get three cookies. 3 x 3 equals 9. There'd be one cookie left over. What if you counted yourself in the problem? Now there are ten cookies to be divided among four people. Each person would get two cookies and there'd be two left over. This is called leaving a **remainder**. A remainder is what remains when a number does not divide evenly.

Let's say you've got 19 cookies to divide among 5 friends.

$$5\overline{)19}$$

How many 5s are in 1? None, so move to the next whole number. How many 5s are in 19? There is room for three 5s in 19.

Subtract to find how many are left.

$$5\overline{)\begin{array}{r} 3 \\ 19 \\ \underline{15} \\ 4 \end{array}}$$

Hmmm, 5 isn't going to divide into 4 evenly no matter what we do. So 4 is the remainder. This is usually written 3 r 4.

For the extra special gold star, how about if you divide 4 by 5 anyway—what the heck, be wild and crazy.

$$5\overline{)4}$$

How many groups of 5 are there in 4? None. And how many are left over? Well, the original 4 you tried to divide into never got divided, so that 4 is still left over. So, the answer is, 0 r 4. Also known as, zero remainder four.

Ready for a tougher one? Let's take a couple of ugly numbers, the kind you just know aren't going to work out. Let's divide 714 by 17. It's a tough job, but somebody's got to do it. The truth is, this division problem will be a breeze if we just take it step by step.

$$17\overline{)714}$$

First, how many groups of 17 will fit in 7? None, 7 is not big enough, so try 71. Can groups of 17 fit into 71? Sure they can. How many? Well, here is where your approximating skills will make life easier. Really, 17 is approximately 20, and 71 is approximately 70. Twenty can fit into 70 about three times with a little more left over The first number you are going to try on top is 3.

$$\frac{3}{17\overline{)714}}$$

Try the multiplication down, does it work?

$$
\begin{array}{r}
3 \\
17\overline{)714} \\
51 \\
\hline
20
\end{array}
$$

Now look at the number you have subtracted, 20. It's bigger than 17, right? You can squeeze another group of 17 out of there, can't you? This means that 3 is too small, you need to try another number. Erase the 3 and try the next biggest number, which is 4.

$$
\begin{array}{r}
4 \\
17\overline{)714} \\
68 \\
\hline
3
\end{array}
$$

Much better; now drop the 4 from the end of 714, and you have 34.

$$
\begin{array}{r}
42 \\
17\overline{)714} \\
68 \\
\hline
34
\end{array}
$$

How many times does 17 go into 34? Exactly two. Put that up on top and multiply to check it.

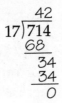

$$
\begin{array}{r}
42 \\
17\overline{)714} \\
68 \\
\hline
34 \\
34 \\
\hline
0
\end{array}
$$

Perfect. 714 divided by 17 is exactly 42. By the way, that number 42, the answer to the problem, is called the **quotient**. A quotient is simply a fancy name for the result of a division problem.

✍ QUIZ D ✍
Division Review

1. $3\overline{)6}$

2. $3\overline{)24}$

3. $3\overline{)28}$

4. $6\overline{)132}$

5. $12\overline{)132}$

6. Sondra has eight pictures she wants to hang on the four walls of her room, and she wants each wall to have the same number of pictures. How many pictures will each wall have?

7. Taylor has thirty-two bugs in his bug collection. He wants to arrange them on eight velvet display boards, with each board having the same number of bugs. How many bugs will be on each board?

8. Jennifer has three friends over to tea, and she has made thirty-five sandwiches (she was feeling a trifle hungry). If she and her three friends are to get an equal numbers of sandwiches, how many will each of them get, and will any be left over? (And if any are left over, how many?)

9. Taylor has two hundred and twenty-five shirts, but only nine shirt drawers. If every drawer must have the same number of shirts, (his parents are real sticklers for neatness) how many shirts will each drawer have?

10. Jennifer has agreed to visit the local children's hospital, and distribute her absolutely cool animal teeth collection. She has three-hundred and fifty-two teeth in the collection, including shark and bear teeth, and there are sixteen sick kids in the hospital. If she promised to give each kid the same number of teeth, how many teeth will each kid get? And, just to approximate before you do the problem, will they get more or fewer than twenty each?

THINK ABOUT THIS

You can tell if a number is divisible by 3 by adding up that number's digits and seeing if they form a number divisible by three. If they do, the original number is divisible by 3.

Glossary

Acute: An angle measuring less than 90°.

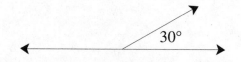

Add: To combine numbers or objects.

Angle: The shape created when two lines intersect.

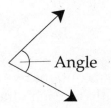

Approximation: Guessing the size or amount of a number or group of things.

Area: The surface covered by a shape.

Associative Law of Addition: A law that says the numbers in an addition problem will always add up to the same amount no matter how they are grouped.

Average or arithmetic mean: A number expressing the norm of a group of numbers.

Axes: The horizontal and vertical lines on which the measurements of a graph are marked. The horizontal line is called the *x*-axis and the veritcal is called *y*-axis.

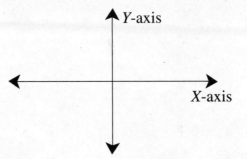

Base: The bottom side of a shape.

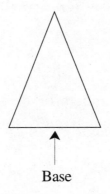

Base

Bimodal: A sample that contains two modes, or two numbers that occur as frequently as each other and more frequently than the other numbers in the sample.

Borrow: To use the value of the digit to the left of the one being subtracted from to make subtraction easier.

$$\begin{array}{r} {}^{0}\!\!{}^{1}\!\!5 \\ -\,9 \\ \hline 6 \end{array}$$

Bow tie: A method of adding or subtracting fractions.

Cancellation: The process of finding common factors in the numerators and denominators of two fractions being multiplied, and dividing the numerator and denominator of the different fractions by this factor to make multiplication easier.

$$\frac{4}{3} \times \frac{9}{2} = \frac{6}{1} \qquad \frac{\overset{2}{\cancel{4}}}{\underset{1}{\cancel{3}}} \times \frac{\overset{3}{\cancel{9}}}{\underset{1}{\cancel{2}}} = \frac{6}{1} = \boxed{6}$$

Carrying: The process of bringing over a digit's value to the next column an addition problem.

$$\overset{1}{15}$$
$$\underline{+\,9}$$
$$24$$

Cent: A root of many words in English. It means 100.

Circle: A closed two-dimensional shape, perfectly round.

Circle graph: A graph showing a whole divided into parts with a circle cut into percentages.

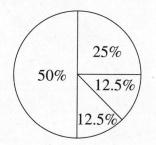

Circumference: The outside border of a circle.

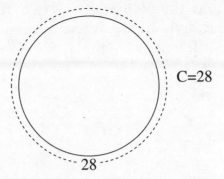

C=28

28

Coefficient: The number in front of a variable and by which the variable is multiplied. In $4x$ for example, 4 is the coefficient of x, and the expression means "4 times x."

Combinations: Possible ways to combine various objects or possibilities, without regard to the order in which they are to be combined.

Common denominator: A denominator that is a multiple of all fraction denominators in a particular addition or subtraction problem.

Commutative Law of Addition: A law that says when you add numbers, the result is the same no matter what order those numbers are in.

Commutative Law of Multiplication: A law that says the result of multiplication will be the same no matter what order the numbers are in.

Cone: A closed, three-dimensional shape starting at a circle and narrowing to a point.

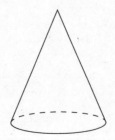

Congruent: The math word for shapes that are exactly equal.

Cross-multiplying: Multiplying diagonally across an equal sign in order to find a missing value.

Cube: A closed, six-sided, three-dimensional shape with six equal sides and twelve equal edges, and every angle a right angle. (A square box.)

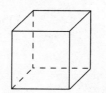

Cubic units: Units in the shape of cubes used to measure the volume of three-dimensional figures.

Cylinder: A three-dimensional closed tube, with equal circles at either end.

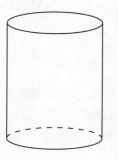

Decimal: A fraction written as a number to the right of the decimal point, with a denominator that is a power of 10.

Decimal point: The point to the direct right of the units digit in a number.

9.1234

↑

Decimal point

Denominator: The bottom part of a fraction.

$$\frac{1}{2} \longleftarrow \text{Denominator}$$

Diagonal: A line that passes from one vertex of a shape to the one opposite, directly through the center of the shape.

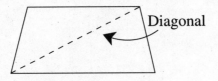

Diameter: A line drawn through the center of a circle from one side to the other.

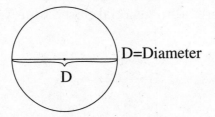

Diamond: A closed, four-sided, two-dimensional shape with two sets of equal angles: an obtuse pair of angles opposite one another, and an acute pair opposite one another.

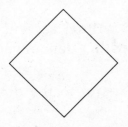

Digit: A number between 0 and 9.

Digit places: The spaces in a number occupied by digits. Which spaces the digits are in give the number its value.

Dimension: The measurement of a geometric shape.

Distributive Law: A law that says multiplying two numbers is the same as multiplying one of the numbers by two numbers that add up to the other number, and adding these products. Also known as: a(b + c) = ab + ac.

Divisible: When a number can be divided into equal parts by another number, with no remainder, that number is divisible.

Division: A way of separating a number into equal groups.

Equation: A complete mathematical expression containing an equal sign. The equals sign means that the expressions on either side of the sign are equivalent, that is, they ultimately represent the same number.

Equilateral triangle: A triangle with three equal sides and three equal angles.

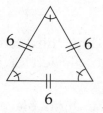

Even: A number that can be divided by 2 with no remainder.

Exponent: A small floating number telling you to multiply the base number times itself a certain number of times.

$$2^{③} \leftarrow \text{Exponent}$$

Extremes: The outside numbers expressed in a proportion.

$$3 : 2 :: 6 : 4$$
Extremes

Factors: Numbers that multiply to produce a certain product. For instance, 2 and 3 are factors of 6.

Fraction: A number expressed as part over whole, with a fraction bar.

Height: The length of a line drawn from the top of a shape to form a right angle with the base.

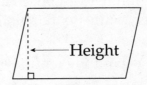

Hexagon: A closed, two-dimensional, six-sided shape.

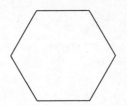

Hundreds digit: The digit third from the right in a whole number, and three to the left of the decimal point in a decimal.

Hundredths place: The digits place two to the right of the decimal point.

9.1234
↑
Hundredths place

Hypotenuse: The side opposite the right angle in a right triangle.

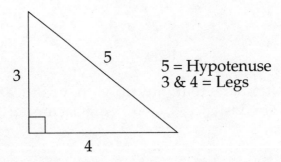

Independent events: Events whose outcomes have no effect on each other.

Infinite or ∞ :   Without end.

Intersection: The meeting of lines.

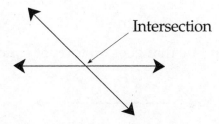

Intersection

Improper fraction: A fraction in which the top part is larger than the bottom part.

Isolating the variable: Manipulating a mathematical expression so that the variable is all alone on one side of the equal sign.

Isosceles triangle: A triangle with two equal sides and two equal angles opposite those sides.

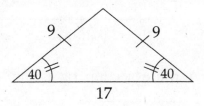

Legs: The shorter sides of a right triangle.

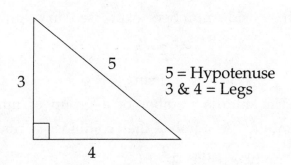

5 = Hypotenuse
3 & 4 = Legs

Length: The longer dimension of the side of a quadrilateral.

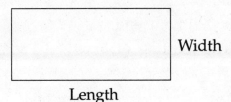

Width

Length

Line: A straight line that goes on forever connecting at least two points.

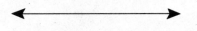

Line graph: A graph made of a horizontal and a vertical axis, expressing the relationship between two different scales.

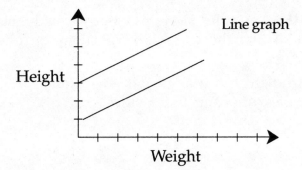

Line graph

Height

Weight

Line segment: A finite section of a line.

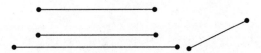

Means: The inside numbers expressed in a proportion.

$$3 : 2 :: 6 : 4$$

Means

Median: The middle number of a group of numbers.

Mixed number: A number that combines a fraction and a whole number, like $2\frac{2}{3}$.

Mode: The most frequently occurring number in a group of numbers.

Multiple: The product of a number multiplied by any whole number. For instance, 12 is a multiple of 6.

Multiply: A quick way of adding a number to itself a given certain number of times. Can be within as 2×3, (2)(3), $2 \bullet 3$, or 2(3).

Negative number: A number less than 0.

Numerator: The top part of a fraction.

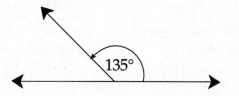

Obtuse: An angle measuring more than 90°.

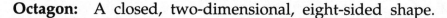

Octagon: A closed, two-dimensional, eight-sided shape.

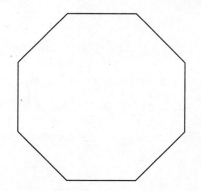

Odd: A number that cannot be evenly divided by 2.

Order of Operations: The specific order—parentheses, exponents, multiplication, division, addition, subtraction—in which to do arithmetic problems.

Parallel: Lines that run together but remain an equal distance apart, never intersecting.

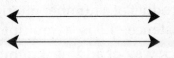

Parallelogram: A quadrilateral with two pairs of parallel sides.

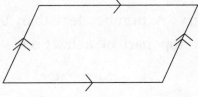

Parentheses or **( ):** Punctuation marks surrounding parts of a math problem that usually indicate the part of the problem you address first.

PEMDAS: An acronym for the specific order in which to do arithmetic problems: parentheses, exponents, multiplication, division, addition, subtraction. Also known as: Please Excuse My Dear Aunt Sally.

Pentagon: A closed, two-dimensional, five-sided shape.

Percent or **%:** A way of expressing the amount per 100.

Perimeter: The length of the outside border of a closed shape.

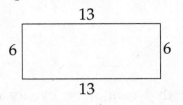

$$P = 6 + 13 + 6 + 13 = 38$$

Permutations: Possible arrangements of a group of objects or possibilities.

Perpendicular: Two lines that meet to form right angles.

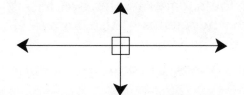

Pi or π: The ratio of the circumference of any circle to its diameter.

Pictograph: A graph showing information with little pictures.

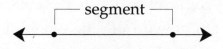

Planar: Flat (two-dimensional.)

Point: A mark taking up no space.

Positive number: A number greater than 0.

Power: The result of raising a number to an exponent.

Prime number: A number that has no factors other than itself and 1. 2, 3, 5, 7, 11, 13, 17, 19 are examples of prime numbers. The number 1 is not prime.

Probability: The likelihood that something will happen, often expressed as a fraction.

Product: The result of multiplication.

Proportion: The expression of the increase or decrease of a ratio.

Protractor: An instrument used to measure the number of degrees in an angle.

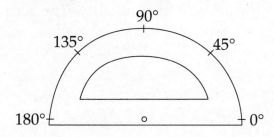

Pythagorean Theorem: A law that says in a right triangle, the sum of the squares of the two legs is equal to the square of the hypotenuse. Also known as: $a^2 + b^2 = c^2$, where c is the hypothenuse.

Quadrilateral: A closed, two-dimensional, four-sided shape.

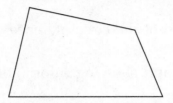

Quotient: The result of a division problem.

Radius: A length drawn from the center of a circle to the edge.

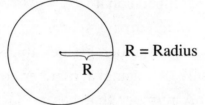

Ratio: An expression showing the relative parts of a whole. A ratio of 2 to 3 can be shown as 2 : 3, or 2 to 3, or $\frac{2}{3}$.

Ratio box: A box used to help figure out answers to ratio questions.

Ray: A line beginning at a fixed point that then goes to infinity.

Reciprocal: The inverse of a number. The reciprocal of 5 is $\frac{1}{5}$.

Rectangle: A closed, four-sided, two-dimensional shape with four right angles.

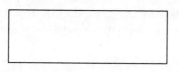

Reducing: The method of putting a fraction in its simplest form.

Remainder: What is left over when a number does not divide evenly.

Rhombus: A parallelogram with four equal sides.

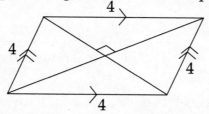

Right angle: An angle of exactly ninety degrees.

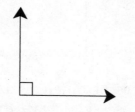

Right triangle: A triangle containing a right angle.

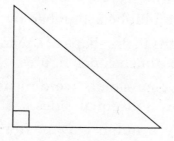

Round: To increase or cut off the end of a number to give it an approximate value.

Scale: An expression of the ratio of information to the lines on a graph, given in the graph.

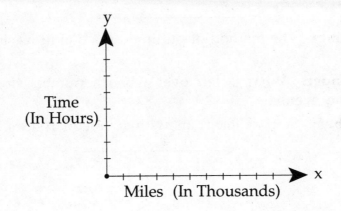

Side: The edge of a closed two-dimensional shape.

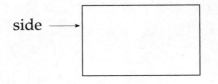

Similar: Two shapes of different sizes whose angles are the same and whose sides have the exact same ratio.

Sphere: A perfectly round, closed, three-dimensional globe.

Square, To: To multiply a number by itself.

Square units: Units in the shape of squares used to measure the area of two-dimensional figures.

Squares: Closed, four-sided, two-dimensional shapes with four right angles and equal sides.

Subtract: To take a number away from another.

Sum: The result of addition.

Tens digit: The digit second from the right on a whole number, and two to the left of the decimal point in a decimal.

67.0
↑
Tens digit

Tenths place: The digits place directly to the right of the decimal point.

9.1234
↑
Tenths place

Thousandths place: The digits place three to the right of the decimal point.

9.1234
↑
Thousandths place

Three-dimensional: Taking up space or volume; not flat.

Times: Another way of saying "multiplied by."

Trapezoid: A quadrilateral with two parallel sides, and two non-parallel sides.

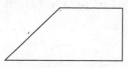

Triangles: Closed, three-sided, two-dimensional shapes.

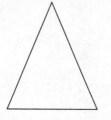

Two-dimensional: Flat.

Units digit: The digit furthest to the right on a whole number, and the first digit to the left of the decimal point in a decimal.

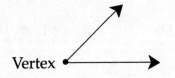

Units digit

Variable: A letter that represents a number in an algebraic equation.

Vertex: The point or corner of an angle.

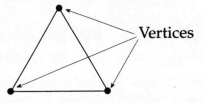

Vertices: The plural of vertex; points or corners of a shape or group of angles.

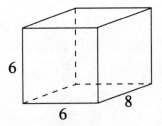

Volume: The amount of space taken up by a three-dimensional shape.

$$V = L \times W \times H = 8 \times 6 \times 6 = 288$$

Width: The shorter dimension of the side of a quadrilateral.

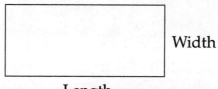

Width

Length

X-axis: The horizontal axis of a graph.

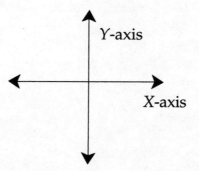

Y-axis: The vertical axis of a graph.

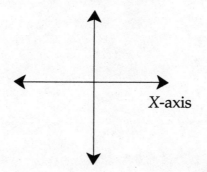

Answers

✍ QUIZ A ✍
Addition Review

1. 44

2. 134

3. 612

4. 399

5. 4,657

6. 35
   Well, 13 kittens plus 22 kittens is the same as
   13 + 22. And 13 + 22 = 35.

7. 141 race cars
   Remember, the word "altogether" should have
   tipped you off that this was an addition problem.
   28 + 113 = 141

8. 28 days absent
   2 + 17 + 9 = 28

9. 148 stamps
   32 + 49 + 67 = 148

10. 323 sea shells
    12 + 31 + 17 + 263 = 323

✍ QUIZ B ✍
Subtraction Review

1. 15

2. 33

3. 112
   You had to borrow here. If it gave you trouble,
   go back to the borrowing section on page 168.

4. 105

    You had to borrow here, too.

5. 894

    Did you approximate first and realize that the
    answer had to be around 900?

6. 14

    39 − 25 = 14

7. 11

    23 − 12 = 11

8. 93

    225 − 132 = 93 This may have been tough, be-
    cause you were trying to find out the difference
    and you may not have known it was subtraction.
    But whenever you are looking for the difference
    between two numbers, subtraction is the way to
    find it.

9. 78

    117 − 39 = 78 Here you had to borrow, and it
    might have gotten complicated. But to check your
    work, just add back. Does the answer plus 39
    equal 117? If not, you need to change it.

10. 872

    40 + 100 = 140 detective novels and science
    fiction. Then, out of 1,012, well, 1,012 − 140 =
    872.

✍ QUIZ C ✍
Multiplication Review

1. 42

2. 40

3. 140

    Did you remember that to multiply by 10, you
    just add a 0 to the end of the number?

4. 322

    Did you approximate first? Try 23 times 10 is
    230, and 23 times 20 is about 400, so 23 times 14
    is somewhere in between those two.

5. 10

6. 10 books
   $2 \times 5 = 10$

7. 70 jelly beans
   $10 \times 7 = 70$

8. 100 spiders
   $10 \times 10 = 100$. Remember, just add a 0

9. 726 race cars
   $22 \times 33 = 726$. How close was your approximation?

10. 4,429 centipede legs total
    $103 \times 43 = 4,429$. To approximate, try 40 times 100. Since you multiply by 100, add two 0s instead of the one 0 you add with 10. A 40 with two 0s is 4,000, way more than 1,000.

✍ QUIZ D ✍
Division Review

1. 2

2. 8

3. 9 r 1.
   Because $3 \times 9 = 27$, and then the extra 1 of 28 is the remainder.

4. 22

5. 11

6. 2 pictures on each wall
   You could even draw a picture of this room and the walls if that makes it easier for you. Eight pictures divided among 4 walls is $8 \div 4$, which equals 2.

7. 4 bugs per board
   Whenever you have trouble deciding which number is being divided into, ask yourself which amount is being separated into groups. The 32 bugs are being divided among 8 boards, so $32 \div 8$, which is equal to 4.

8. **8 sandwiches each, with 3 left over**
   There are 35 sandwiches and 4 people eating
   (Sondra *and* her 3 friends). The sandwiches are
   being divided up among the friends, so 4 ÷ 35,
   which equals 8 r 3.

9. **25 shirts per drawer**
   The 225 shirts are being separated into groups to
   be put into drawers. So, 225 ÷ 9.

10. **Each child will get 22 teeth.**
    How can you approximate here? Well, about 350
    teeth, about 15 kids, if each kid got 10 teeth
    that's 150, so twice that, or 20 teeth each, is
    about 300. There are more teeth than 300, right?
    So each kid will get more than 20. 352 ÷ 16 = 22.

✍ QUIZ #1 ✍
Arithmetic Check

1. **29, an odd number**
   Since this problem has addition and subtraction
   only, you do it in the order it appears, left to
   right. So, 17 + 34 = 51, and 51 − 22 = 29. Can
   you divide 29 evenly into two groups? Nope, so
   29 is odd.

2. **205, an odd number and *not* a multiple of 3**
   This is a little tricky unless you remember the
   order of operations. Multiplication and division
   come before addition and subtraction, so the first
   thing to do is the multiplication, 100 × 3 = 300.
   Then the subtraction, 505 − 300 = 205. Is it divisible into two equal groups? No, so it is odd.
   Add up the digits, 2 + 0 + 5 = 7. Is 7 divisible
   by 3? No, so the number 205 is not divisible by 3.

3. **138, which is even, and is not a multiple of 5. It
   is also not prime.**
   Whew, this one looked scary! But if you just held
   on and relaxed, it wasn't so bad. First, multiplication and division left to right, so 20 × 3 = 60,
   then 60 ÷ 4 = 15. Then addition and subtraction
   left to right, 15 + 23 + 17 + 83 = 138. Since 138

ends in an even number, it is even, and since it does not end in 5 or 0 it is not divisible by 5. How do you know whether it is prime? Well, it is divisible by 2, isn't it, because it's even? So that means 2 is one of its factors, and a prime number can only have two factors, itself and 1, so 138 is not prime.

4. 181, which is not a multiple of 5. And 181 divided by 3, the answer is 60 r 1.
    Are you getting the hang of these yet? The division and multiplication always comes first and goes left to right, so 234 ÷ 6 = 39, and 39 × 2 = 78. Then the addition, 78 + 103 = 181. Does 181 end in 5 or 0? No, so it is not a multiple of 5. Divide 181 by 3 and you get 60 r 1.

5. 725, which is a multiple of 5, but it is neither a multiple of 3, nor is it prime.
    Multiplication and division first, right? So, 309 × 25 = 7,725. Then, 7,725 ÷ 15 = 515, then you have 200 + 515 + 10 = 725. This is a multiple of 5 because it ends in 5, but 7 + 2 + 5 = 14, and 14 is not divisible by 3, so 725 is not divisible by 3. Is it prime? Well, you know it is divisible by 5, so 5 is a factor of 725, and this 725 has more factors than just itself and 1, so it is *not* prime.

6. 8 autographed baseballs
    Because 37 − 29 = 8.

7. 75 strawberries
    Each basket has 25 berries, and 3 times that means the problem should read, 25 × 3, which equals 75.

8. 2 ice cream sandwiches each, with 2 left over
    Sondra and her 11 friends make up a total of 12 people sharing in this pool of 26 ice cream sandwiches. So, 12 ÷ 26 is 2 remainder 2.

9. 6,526 pounds of books
    That's a lot of books. This is a multiplication problem; he does a load of 251 twenty-six times, so 251 × 26 = 6,526.

10. **36 maps, with 6 dollars left over**

This is a little bit more complicated, but it uses the same operations you've been using the whole time. First, how much money does Jennifer have? Each of 14 relatives gave her 39 dollars, so 14 × 39 = 546 dollars. Now, she needs to know how many groups of 15 dollars she can get out of the 546 dollars. So, she divides the 546 into groups of 15. 546 ÷ 15, this goes in 36 times, with 6 left over at the bottom. So she could buy 36 maps and still have 6 dollars left for something else.

✍ QUIZ #2 ✍
Fractions

1. $\dfrac{2}{5}$

There are a total of 5 pieces in the whole, and 2 of them are shaded, so 2 is the part over the whole of 5.

2. $\dfrac{1}{5}$

There are 10 parts to the whole, and 2 of them are shaded, so the fraction is $\dfrac{2}{10}$. To reduce this fraction, divide both the top and the bottom by 2:

$$\frac{2 \div 2}{10 \div 2} = \frac{1}{5}.$$

3. $\dfrac{3}{4} + \dfrac{1}{5} = \dfrac{19}{20}$

Whew! The pie in the picture has 12 of 16 parts shaded. So, $\dfrac{12}{16}$ can be reduced, first by 2, to $\dfrac{6}{8}$, then by 2 again, to $\dfrac{3}{4}$. Or you could have reduced by 4, either is fine. Then, the answer to question 2 was $\dfrac{1}{5}$. $\dfrac{1}{5} + \dfrac{3}{4}$ you can bow tie, and the answer is $\dfrac{19}{20}$. Then there is that tricky part—the answer cannot be reduced! Sorry if it threw you.

4. $\dfrac{21}{10} = 2\dfrac{1}{10}$

To subtract mixed numbers, convert them to improper fractions first. So, $3\dfrac{1}{2}$ becomes $\dfrac{7}{2}$, and $1\dfrac{2}{5}$ becomes $\dfrac{7}{5}$, and the question looks like this: $\dfrac{7}{2} - \dfrac{7}{5}$. Then you can use the bow tie. When you are done take a look at the question again. Could you have approximated it?

5. $\dfrac{67}{6}$ or $11\dfrac{1}{6}$

Same as the one you just looked at, to add mixed numbers, convert them to improper fractions. So, $9\dfrac{2}{3}$ becomes $\dfrac{29}{3}$ and $1\dfrac{1}{2}$ becomes $\dfrac{3}{2}$. $\dfrac{29}{3} + \dfrac{3}{2} = \dfrac{67}{6}$. Then, convert to a mixed number: 6 goes into 67 11 times, with 1 left over.

6. $\dfrac{3}{4}$

Draw a picture to see how this works. Divide the pie into 4, so there are quarters, then shade in the quarter of Rose's, and the 2 other quarters of her friends. Altogether, that is 3 parts of the pie out of a possible 4, so $\dfrac{3}{4}$.

7. $\dfrac{4}{4}$, better known as 1 whole bag of candy

He starts out with $\dfrac{1}{4}$, then adds $\dfrac{2}{4}$ and another $\dfrac{1}{4}$. Since you already have a common denominator, just add the numerators. $1 + 2 + 1 = 4$, and $\dfrac{4}{4}$, just like any number over itself, is equal to 1.

8. $\dfrac{16}{35}$

Sondra had $\dfrac{6}{7}$, and her sister took $\dfrac{2}{5}$. To subtract, use the bow tie. $\dfrac{6}{7} - \dfrac{2}{5} = \dfrac{16}{35}$

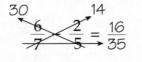

$\dfrac{16}{35}$ is less than half, but just barely. How can you tell? Well, one way is to look at the numerator (16). Is it half of the denominator (35)? Not quite; it's less.

9. $\dfrac{51}{6}$ or $\dfrac{17}{2}$ or $8\dfrac{1}{2}$ checker sets.

To add mixed numbers, convert them to improper fractions! $3\dfrac{2}{3} + 4\dfrac{5}{6}$ becomes $\dfrac{11}{3} + \dfrac{29}{6}$. Then, you can bow tie, or ask yourself, is one denominator a multiple of another? Yes, 6 is multiple of 3, so you can just transform $\dfrac{11}{3}$ by multiplying it by $\dfrac{2}{2}$ to become $\dfrac{22}{6}$. Then, $\dfrac{22}{6} + \dfrac{29}{6} = \dfrac{51}{6}$. Reduce or make into a mixed number.

10. $\dfrac{45}{8}$ or $5\dfrac{5}{8}$

Transform to a fraction, then subtract: $10\dfrac{3}{4}$ becomes $\dfrac{43}{4}$, and $3\dfrac{7}{8}$ becomes $\dfrac{41}{8}$. Can you see an easy common denominator without the bow tie? Sure, 8 is a multiple of 4, so $\dfrac{43}{4}\times\dfrac{2}{2}$ becomes $\dfrac{86}{8}$. Then $\dfrac{86}{8}-\dfrac{41}{8}=\dfrac{45}{8}$. And no, she didn't have quite enough fake blood after the spill.

✍ QUIZ #3 ✍
Multiplying and Dividing Fractions

1. $\dfrac{1}{6}$

To multiply fractions, just multiply the tops and the bottoms straight across.

2. $\dfrac{2}{45}$

3. 1

Did you realize that this can be written $\dfrac{\frac{1}{2}}{\frac{1}{2}}$? Any number over itself is equal to 1.

4. $\dfrac{7}{3}$

Just convert the mixed numbers to fractions. Then you can cancel. $\dfrac{7}{2}\times\dfrac{2}{3}=\dfrac{7}{3}$.

5. $\dfrac{30}{47}$

Once you convert these to improper fractions and flip them over, you can cancel and multiply.

6. $4\dfrac{4}{5}$

To make this easier, you need to first figure out what the problem is asking. The question is asking how many bags will he give away? Well, in a way, the answer is right there: It says he will give away $\dfrac{4}{5}$ of the marbles he has, or $\dfrac{4}{5}$ of 6. You know that when you see the word "of," it means multiply, so $\dfrac{4}{5} \times 6 = \dfrac{24}{5}$. Remember, 6 can just be written as $\dfrac{6}{1}$ to make the problem easier to look at. And, of course, the answer will be less than 6 because the question is asking for a fractional part of 6.

7. 28

This question asks how many slices exist within the pizza she has, so it is really asking you to divide the pizza she has into slices. Divide is the operative word here. So the $\dfrac{7}{8}$ pizza is being divided into slices, $\dfrac{1}{32}$. $\dfrac{7}{8} \div \dfrac{1}{32}$ becomes $\dfrac{7}{8} \times \dfrac{32}{1}$. Can you cancel now that you have flipped it? Certainly: $\dfrac{7}{1} \times \dfrac{4}{1} = 28$.

$$\dfrac{7}{\cancel{8}_1} \times \dfrac{\cancel{32}^{4}}{1} = \dfrac{28}{1} = 28$$

8. $\dfrac{1}{15}$

What word in this problem tips you off that it is a multiplication problem? The word "of," as in "he wants to give his brother $\dfrac{1}{3}$ of it." So, $\dfrac{1}{5} \times \dfrac{1}{3} = \dfrac{1}{15}$.

9. $\dfrac{7}{10}$

Again you see the word "of" in "She wants to take $\dfrac{1}{5}$ of their cantalope stash," and you know you are dealing with a multiplication problem. So, convert that mixed number to a fraction and you have $\dfrac{7}{2} \times \dfrac{1}{5} = \dfrac{7}{10}$. This is less than 1, and you could have approximated to yourself, "Well, one fifth, hmmm, if they had 5 that means she would take 1, since they have less than 5 she will probably take less than 1."

10. $\dfrac{112}{5}$ or $22\dfrac{2}{5}$

You probably knew this was a division problem by the way the question asked, "How many are contained in her collection?" So convert $5\dfrac{3}{5}$ to a fraction, $\dfrac{28}{5}$ and divide by $\dfrac{1}{4}$. As long as you didn't make the deadly mistake of canceling before you flipped over the second fraction, you should have ended with $\dfrac{28}{5} \times \dfrac{4}{1} = \dfrac{112}{5}$.

1. $\dfrac{3}{6}$ and $\dfrac{1}{2}$ are equal. The others reduce to $\dfrac{1}{5}$, $\dfrac{2}{3}$, and $\dfrac{2}{5}$.

2. $\dfrac{5}{6}$

Use the bow tie!

3. $\dfrac{9}{8}$ or $1\dfrac{1}{8}$

Just invert the second fraction and multiply. *Never cancel in a division problem before you invert the fraction!*

4. $\dfrac{11}{8}$ or $1\dfrac{3}{8}$

Convert $3\dfrac{2}{3}$ to a fraction and multiply straight across. It becomes $\dfrac{3}{8}\times\dfrac{11}{3}$, and here you can cancel because the question is in multiplication form.

$$\dfrac{\overset{1}{\cancel{3}}}{8} \times \dfrac{11}{\underset{1}{\cancel{3}}} = \dfrac{11}{8} = \dfrac{11}{8}.$$

5. $\dfrac{7}{11}$

Convert to fractions, invert the second one, and multiply. You get $\dfrac{7}{11}\times\dfrac{2}{11}$, and the 2s cancel.

6. No.

Does $\dfrac{2}{3}$ equal $\dfrac{3}{6}$? Well, see if the fractions are in their most reduced forms. Do 2 and 3 have any common multiples? Nope, so $\frac{2}{3}$ is in its most reduced form. Do 3 and 6 have any common multiples? Yes, they are both divisible by 3, so you can reduce $\frac{3}{6}$; it becomes $\frac{1}{2}$. Does $\frac{2}{3}=\frac{1}{2}$? Nope. You can also draw a picture: divide a circle into 3 parts and shade in 2 of them for the $\frac{2}{3}$. Then draw a circle the same size, divide it into 2 parts, and shade in 1 of them for the $\frac{1}{2}$. Is the same amount shaded both times? No way, so the fractions are not equal.

7. $\frac{1}{6}$

The key to recognizing this as a multiplication problem is the word "of" in "I want $\frac{1}{3}$ *of* those dominoes." Those dominoes are $\frac{1}{2}$, so $\frac{1}{3}\times\frac{1}{2}=\frac{1}{6}$.

8. She uses $\frac{27}{32}$ of a gallon of glue and has $2\frac{17}{32}$ gallons left.

She uses $\frac{1}{4}$ of the glue, so you multiply: $\frac{27}{8}\times\frac{1}{4}=\frac{27}{32}$. She uses $\frac{27}{32}$ of a gallon of glue. How much will she have left? Well, how much did she start with? $\frac{27}{8}$. So, to find $\frac{27}{8}-\frac{27}{32}$, look at the denominators. Is one a multiple of the other?

Sure, 32 is a multiple of 8. Multiply $\frac{27}{8}$ by $\frac{4}{4}$ and you get $\frac{108}{32}$. So, $\frac{108}{32} - \frac{27}{32} = \frac{81}{32}$, or $2\frac{17}{32}$.

9. $\frac{32}{3}$ or $10\frac{2}{3}$

Taylor is separating his buckets into smaller groups, known to the math-smart among us as dividing. He has $\frac{8}{3}$, and wants to divide them into buckets filled only $\frac{1}{4}$ of the way. So, $\frac{8}{3} \div \frac{1}{4} = \frac{8}{3} \times \frac{4}{1} = \frac{32}{3} = 10\frac{2}{3}$ of those $\frac{1}{4}$ buckets.

10. $\frac{69}{32}$ or $2\frac{5}{32}$

When you see the word "of," you have a multiplication question. So, $5\frac{3}{4} \times \frac{3}{8} = \frac{23}{4} \times \frac{3}{8} = \frac{69}{32}$.

✍ QUIZ #5 ✍
Decimals

1. 200
   The hundreds place is where the 2 is, and the number to the right of it is 3. Is 3 less than 5? It sure is, so the 2 remains a 2.

2. 13.5
   The tenths place is just to the right of the decimal point, and the 5 to the right of the tenths place means the 4 is rounded up 1.

3. 5.8
   The numbers, when rounded, are 2.3 and 3.5, then 2.3 + 3.5 = 5.8.

4. 3.534
   Make sure to line up the decimal places exactly when you subtract.

5. 19.82

    Did you approximate first? Then did you line up the numbers according to their decimal places?

6. 3

    Look at 2.32. The tenths place is directly to the right of the decimal point. If you need a little help in visualizing, think about which place is the one that makes you think of dimes.

7. $6.29

    Just line up the decimal places and add. 3.79 + 2.50

8. $0.34 or $\dfrac{34}{100}$ or $\dfrac{17}{50}$

    Simple subtraction with decimals is just a matter of lining them up! 2.32 − 1.98 = 0.34.
    Since the decimal extends as far as the hundredths place, it is $\dfrac{34}{100}$, then you can reduce.

9. 2.356

    Amazing! The decimal gets shorter when you add! Of course, if you want you can leave that 0 on the end but it isn't necessary.

10. 1.52

    This was tough to get lined up unless you remembered to add the zeroes, especially when you are doing subtraction. 4.30 − 2.78 = 1.52

✍ QUIZ #6 ✍
Multiplying and Dividing Decimals

1. 9.2

    Without decimals, 23 × 4 is 92, then move one space to the left for the one decimal place, and you have 9.2.

2. 1.7

Since you are dividing by 2, put the 3.4 under the division roof and put the decimal point on top.

Then divide.

3. 6.72

Multiply without the decimal points, then count the number of places in the numbers being multiplied, and move that number of spaces from the right to the left of the product.

4. 2

Set up the division first.

$$.9\overline{)1.8}$$

Then, move the decimal point of the number you are dividing by, in this case 0.9, to the right until it is a whole number, in this case 9. Then, move the decimal point of the number being divided into, in this case 1.8, the same number of spaces to the right. Then divide. Presto!

5. 230

You could divide the same way you just did in question 4, or you could set this up as a fraction form of division. $\frac{2.3}{0.01}$, move the decimal points over to make the 0.01 a whole number, just as you would in any other division set up, and you have $\frac{230}{1}$, better known as 230.

6. $13.60

Did you approximate first? Let's hope so, it's an excellent habit to get into. What kind of problem is this? Multiplication. He does this 4 *times*. 3.4 × 4 = 13.6

7. 2.6 ounces of snot per tissue (yuck)
   What type of problem is this? Revolting? No, division. How could you tell? Because he is separating the snot into two groups, also know as dividing it. So, 2 ÷ 5.2 = 2.6

8. 14 groups
   Well, approximately, they would have more than seven because each dollar has more than fifty cents in it. This is a division problem, and you can do it as decimal division. 0.5 ÷ 7 becomes 5 ÷ 70 =14, or convert the decimal to a fraction. $0.5 = \dfrac{5}{10} = \dfrac{1}{2}$, then $7 \div \dfrac{1}{2}$ becomes 7×2. Any way you slice it, the answer comes up as fourteen piles of fifty cents each.

9. Jennifer receives 7.55 pounds of Jell-O on an average day.
   This is another multiplication problem, because we are talking about how many *times* per day, and that *times* the Jell-O per knockout will give you your answer. Was your approximation close to the right answer?

10. 9 teeny tiny glasses!
    She is separating the one glass into many smaller glasses, this means she is dividing up the water. So, 0.05 ÷ 0.45 Move the decimal on the 0.05 over to make it a whole number, move the one on 0.45 over the same amount, and go!

✍ QUIZ #7 ✍
Chapter 4 Review

1. 6.3
   When you are adding decimals, be sure to align the digit places.

2. 0.8
   Did you approximate that the answer would be less than 1? Line them up and subtract, then you're done.

3. 4.8

Multiply as though there is no decimal, then count from the right of the product and put the decimal in.

4. 1.6

Don't forget to place the decimal point in the division answer.

5. 4

Either set up as the regular division and move the decimal point until the 0.6 becomes a whole number, or convert the decimals to fractions and divide the fractions the way you learned in chapter 3.

6. $3.00

Just line up the decimals by the decimal places

$\begin{array}{r} 2.55 \\ +0.45 \\ \hline \end{array}$ and add.

7. $1.88

Line up those digits and subtract away!

8. $2.10

This is actually a multiplication problem. One basket is thirty-five cents, two baskets are two times thirty-five cents, and so on. So, 6×0.35 210, then move the decimal point over two spaces to the left because of the two decimal places of 0.35, and you have 2.10. Is that what you approximated?

9. $11\dfrac{1}{2}$

This is a multiplication problem, a lot like problem 8. So, $2.3 \times 5 = 11.5$, and to express 11.5 as a mixed number, use the 11 as the whole number, and convert the 0.5 to $\dfrac{5}{10}$ to $\dfrac{1}{2}$, and you're home free.

10. 12.7

   If Jennifer wants to divide the feathers, so do you. So 0.5 ÷ 6.35; move the decimal point of point five over one to form a whole number, and move the decimal point of the 6.35 over one as well. Then divide.

✍ QUIZ #8 ✍
Proportions and Ratios

1. 2:3

   Both 4 and 6 are even, so they can be divided by 2. The ratio is then 2 : 3.

2. 12

   Remember, in a proportion set up this way, the outsides will multiply to the same as the insides. So, 2 × ? is equal to 3 × 8. 2 × ? = 24 What times 2 is 24? 12.

3. 15

   Just cross-multiply when a proportion is set up this way. 4 × ? = 5 × 12 4 × ? = 60. Divide both sides by 4 and the missing piece is 15.

4. 8

   Again, just cross-multiply. 3 × ? = 4 × 6 3 × ? = 24 What times 3 is 24? 8.

5. 3

   You can cross-multiply, or you can just eyeball this one. In a one-to-one ratio, there are equal parts of both. If you have three of one thing, you must have three of another.

6. 2:1 or $\dfrac{2}{1}$

   Careful, the question asks what is the ratio of *compact discs* to *cassettes*, not the way it was originally given in the problem. The original was cassettes to CDs, and 4:8. Since you need to reverse it, it is 8:4, or $\dfrac{8}{4}$, then divide both the top and the bottom by 2.

7. 6 cups of water
   You can use a ratio box for this.

Sand	Water	Total Cement
3	2	5
×3	×3	×3
9	6	15

   Once you have found the total of the ratio is 5 by adding the two parts, and you know the real total is 15, you realize the ratio was multiplied by 3. Thus, each part was multiplied by 3. Since there were 2 parts water, 3 times that is 6.

8. 9 tablespoons of flour
   The ratio of water to flour is one to three. Add those parts and you have the total and you can use the ratio box.

Water	Flour	Total
1	3	4
×3	×3	×3
3	9	12

   The total is 4, it was multiplied by 3 to form 12 tablespoons so the parts are multiplied by 3. Flour (3) is multiplied by 3 to become 9. Another way to do this problem is to ask yourself what fractional part of the whole the flour is. Since the whole of the ratio is 4, and the flour is 3 parts of that, the fractional part of the ratio is $\frac{3}{4}$. Now, of twelve cups, how much is flour? $\frac{3}{4} \times 12 = 9$

9. 14
   Try the ratio box. The two-to-one ratio adds up to 3. What is 3 multiplied by to become 21? Yep, 7.

Non-fiction	Fiction	Total
1	2	3
×7	×7	×7
7	14	21

So the 2 parts that are fiction books are also multiplied by 7 to become 14. Could you have done this by transforming the ratio into a fraction? Sure, $\frac{2}{3} \times 21 = 14$.

10. 4 gallons of hot fudge

Try a ratio box. You multiply by 4 to get the 16 gallons, so the 1 part fudge is also multiplied by 4.

✍ QUIZ #9 ✍
Conversion

1. 0.5 and 50%

2. 0.75 and 75%

   Just multiply by $\frac{3}{4}$ by $\frac{25}{25}$ to get $\frac{75}{100}$.

3. $\frac{2}{5}$ (reduced from $\frac{4}{10}$) and 40%

4. 0.3 and $\frac{3}{10}$

5. 0.2 and $\frac{1}{5}$ (reduced from $\frac{2}{10}$)

6. 0.29 and $\frac{29}{100}$

7. 0.7 and 70%

   Remember, if the decimal is only in the tenths spot, just throw a 0 into the hundredths slot for your percentage.

8. 0.06 and 6%

   This becomes $\frac{6}{100}$, so the 6 goes in the hundreths slot and a 0 goes in the tenths spot.

9. $\frac{23}{100}$ and 23%

10. $\frac{1}{1,000}$ and 0.1%

    Yuck! Just bear in mind, to transform a decimal to a percent, move the decimal point two spaces over to the right and add a percent sign. All it means here is that you have a fractional percentage.

✍ QUIZ #10 ✎
Percentages

1. 5

   To find 10% of a number, just move the decimal point of that number one space to the left.

2. 4

   You can easily reduce 25% to $\dfrac{25}{100}$ to $\dfrac{1}{4}$, and then multiply as you would a fraction. $\dfrac{1}{4} \times 16 = 4$.

3. 9

   You can transform the percentage to a fraction, cancel if possible, and then multiply.

   $$\dfrac{3}{100} \times 300 = 9$$

4. 40

   You can cross-multiply: 2,000 = 50 x ? Then divide both sides by 50.

   $$40 = ?$$

   Another way to look at it is to just approximate. Look across the equal sign, 50 was multiplied by what to become 100? By 2, so you must multiply 20 by 2 as well.

5. 10

   Well, you can do a lot of different things here: Reduce $\dfrac{2}{20}$ to $\dfrac{1}{10}$, which is 10%. Or cross-multiply. Or a lot of things. Which way did you choose?

6. 1

   Careful! The question wants to know how many she has *left*, not how many she gave away. Then, all you have to figure out is 90% of 10.

$$90\% = \frac{90}{100} = \frac{9}{10}$$

$\frac{9}{10} \times 10 = 9$, which means one left. Or, since she gave away 90%, she kept 10%. What is 10% of 10? Move the decimal point over one space to the left; ten percent of ten is one.

7. $320

Set up your multiplication when you see the word "of."

$$\frac{32}{100} \times 1,000 = 320$$

8. 0

Aren't you shocked? Taylor, who is so sweet to his friends, turns out to be an utter creep when he deals with his brother. Well, not a total creep. Because if his brother is math-smart at all, he knows that anything times zero—and "of" means times—is zero.

9. 10%

You can set this up as a proportion.

$$\frac{3}{30} = \frac{?}{100}$$

Then cross-multiply. Or you can reduce $\frac{3}{30}$, to make life easier, to $\frac{1}{10}$. And $\frac{1}{10}$ is 10%.

10. 0.5% or $\frac{1}{2}$%

Tricky question! Did you get caught? Set the question up as a proportion.

$$\frac{1}{200} = \frac{?}{100}$$

Then, cross-multiply. 200 x ? = 100. You get $\frac{1}{2}$, so the answer is one-half of a percent.

1. $\frac{1}{5}$ and 0.2

   The decimal part is easy. Move the decimal two to the left and drop the percent sign. Then you can set 20% up as a fraction over 100, as all percents are, and reduce.

$$20\% = \frac{20}{100} = \frac{1}{5}$$

2. 12

   Cross-multiply. 24 = 2 × ? Two times 12 is 24.

3. 6

   A proportion has extremes (the outsides) that multiply to form means (the insides).

$$1 \times ? = 2 \times 3$$

   1 × ? = 6 What times 1 is equal to 6? Six times 1 is equal to 6.

4. 0.25 and 25%

   First, transform $\frac{1}{4}$ to a fraction over 100.

$$\frac{1}{4} \times \frac{25}{25} = \frac{25}{100}$$

   Since the number now has a denominator of 100, you can put it in the hundredths place of the decimal (0.25) move the decimal two to the right, and add a percentage sign for the percent.

5. 0.15 and 15%

   First it becomes a fraction with a denominator of 100, $\frac{15}{100}$, then it easily becomes a decimal in the hundredths place, and then a percentage.

6. 15 cups of ink, and the mixture is 60% ink

   Setting up a ratio box is probably your best bet here.

Water	Ink	Total
2	3	5
×5	×5	×5
10	15	25

The total parts in the writing mixture are 5, which was then multiplied by 5 to become 25 cups. Thus, the ink part is multiplied by 5, and 3 × 5 = 15. To find the percentage you can look to the original ratio. If the ink to water is 3:2, then the total is 5 and the part that is ink is 3. So, $\dfrac{3}{5}$ is the fractional part of the mixture that is ink, and $\dfrac{3}{5} = \dfrac{?}{100}$

$$\frac{3}{5} \times \frac{20}{20} = \frac{60}{100} \text{ or } 60\%$$

7. 28 marbles

You can set this up as a regular multiplication problem. $14\% \times 200 = \dfrac{14}{100} \times 200 = 28$.

8. 12 pints of red food coloring; yellow is 25% of the mixture. First you can set up a ratio box, with the ratio of red to yellow at 3 to 1, and the total at four.

Red	Yellow	Total
3	1	4
×4	×4	×4
12	4	16

Since you want the real total to be 16, you multiply each part by 4, and the 3 parts red become

12. To find the yellow percentage, just use fractional parts from the ratio. The ratio is 3:1 red to yellow, so 4 total and $\frac{1}{4}$ yellow part to whole. Then, $\frac{1}{4} = \frac{25}{100} = 25\%$. You can also just remember that $\frac{1}{4}$ is one quarter, also known among those who carry money as 0.25. Cool, huh?

9. 1:1

Percent, you ask? Well, fifty-fifty means $\frac{1}{2}$ water and $\frac{1}{2}$ salt. So, the parts are each 1 and the whole is 2, so the ratio is 1:1, adding up to a whole of 2.

10. 3

You can use a ratio box again, but they don't give the real whole number, just the real number of cars.

Cars	Trucks	Total
5	1	6
× 3	× 3	× 3
15	3	18

That means the real number of cars is 15, so the 5 parts was multiplied by 3. Multiply everything else by 3 and you have 3 trucks, and a total of 18 vehicles in the set.

✍ QUIZ #12 ✍
Average, Median, Mode

1. 3

You can add them up and divide by 3 because there are three numbers.

$$2 + 3 + 4 = 9, \text{ then } 9 \div 3 = 3$$

But you also might want to notice a nice trick: In any odd-numbered group of consecutive numbers, the average (mean) of the group is the number directly in the middle.

2. 5

Add the 2, then divide by 2.

3. 4

Add them up then divide by 5, as there are five numbers in the group.

4. 3

Line them up in size order: 1, 3, 3, 6, 7. Which number is in the exact middle? 3.

5. 3

The mode is the number that occurs the most frequently. Since 3 appears twice, and those other guys only appear once each, 3 is the mode.

6. 8

To find the average, add up the numbers and divide by how many there are. Here, 3 + 6 + 15 = 24, then 24 divided by 3, the number of days, is 8.

7. 12

You know how to find the average, just add the numbers and divide by how many days there are. So you get 36 divided by 3, which is 12. Now, to find the approximate average of Thursday and Saturday, look at the numbers from those days: 10 and 14. Just to approximate, it doesn't look as though their average would be all that different from 12, and it isn't. If you bother to check, you can find that the average of Thursday and Saturday is exactly 12.

8. 4

Add them all, and don't forget that when it says "Two of them are three dollars each," you must add the three dollars twice.

9. 4

   You can use your incredible multiplication skills here. Three 8-person families is just 3 times 8, or 24, and 4 one-person families are just 4 people. Add them up and you have 28, and where the question says "Seven houses," you can just divide the 28 by 7 and get 4.

10. Average: 24 inches
    Mode: 20 inches
    Median: 25 inches

    Whew! Find the average: add the jump heights then divide by how many jumps there were, five in this case. Then the mode. List the numbers and find the one that occurs most. You might as well list them in size order by the way, because you will have to get to the median next: 20, 20, 25, 26, 29. The number that occurs most frequently is 20, so that is the mode. The median is the number smack dab in the middle, and that is 25.

✍ QUIZ #13 ✍
Probability

1. $\dfrac{1}{5}$

   Probability is determined by the number of successful possibilities over the number of total possibilities. So one green over the 5 total possibilities.

2. $\dfrac{2}{5}$

   Same reasoning as above, except that red is more likely as there are 2 reds, and only 1 green.

3. 0

   It is absolutely certain that you will not select a white Lifesaver as there are none in the bag, so the probability is $\dfrac{0}{5}$ or 0. Good thing too, because the white ones are coconut. Gross.

4. $\dfrac{1}{25}$

This is a little more difficult. To find out how many possibilities there are for two events, you multiply the number of possibilities. So 5 different possibilities for the first, and 5 for the second, and $5 \times 5 = 25$. Then, there is only one way to get 2 greens, so $\dfrac{1}{25}$.

5. $\dfrac{4}{25}$

The probability for orange the first time is $\dfrac{2}{5}$, then the second is $\dfrac{2}{5}$ again. To find the probability of both, multiply and you get $\dfrac{4}{25}$. Or, you can list out the possibilities to check yourself, if you like.

✍ QUIZ #14 ✍

1. 6

You can easily list these out. Or you can say, "How many possibilities for the first one? Three. How many for the second? Two. For the third? One." Then multiply.

$$3 \times 2 \times 1 = 6$$

2. 12

Again, either list or use the math you've learned. How many prizes can be the first prize on the wall? Four. The second? Three. Multiply.

$$4 \times 3 = 12$$

3. 12

This is a combination problem, and you can check back to page 103 to see how to do these if you forgot. How many possibilities for engines? Three. How many hull designs? Two. How many interior designs? Two. Then multiply.

$$3 \times 2 \times 2 = 12$$

4. 12

Eerie! Soon you will think all the answers to combination questions are 12, but it isn't true. Just see how many possibilities there are for each stage: fruit, two; bread, three; cheese, two. Multiply.

$$2\times 3\times 3 =12$$

5. 720

That is a lot of possible combinations; be glad that you don't have to make the decision. You are back to arrangements of possibilities or permutations. How many could be the first move? Ten. The second has nine possibilities, since you have used one of the moves up on the first, and the third has eight, since you have used two of the moves on the first two of the sequence. $10 \times 9 \times 8 = 720$.

✍ QUIZ #15 ✍
Chapter 6 Review

1. 0

There are no green marbles, so it is certain that Rose will not choose one, and the way to express the certainty that an event will not happen is that it has a probability of 0. Or $\dfrac{0}{20}$, which equals 0.

2. $\dfrac{3}{20}$

The number of successful possibilities is 3 for the 3 blue marbles. The number of total possibilities is 20 for the 20 marbles in the bag.

3. Mike

You don't need to compute the average here, just see that Mike ran all of his races in less total time than Grace, so his average time must be less.

4. $\dfrac{1}{2}$

    You can reduce probabilities. There are a total of
    10 balls, and the number of successful possibilities
    is 5, so $\dfrac{5}{10}$ or $\dfrac{1}{2}$. The two probabilities are equal.

5. 1

    Since there are only blue balls in the box, the
    number of successful outcomes is the same as the
    number of possible outcomes, or $\dfrac{10}{10}$ which equals
    1. A probability of 1 means the successful out-
    come is certain.

6. 53 inches

    Add the numbers together, and divide by how
    many numbers there were, in this case, three
    years.

    $$159 \div 3 = 53$$

    Did you also notice that 53 is exactly in the
    middle of an odd group of numbers? You could
    have just chosen it as the average if you thought
    of it, and it is often nice to do less work than
    you might to get the same answer.

7. 18

    Again, here the numbers are an odd group in
    exact order, so you can choose the middle num-
    ber. Or you can add them and divide by how
    many there are.

    $$16 + 18 + 20 = 54, \text{ and } 54 \div 3 = 18.$$

8. 210

    This is a permutation question, so you need to
    figure out the arrangements. How many possibili-
    ties for the first song on the tape? Well, there are
    seven songs on the tape, so there are seven
    possibilities for the first song. Then, there are six

songs left possible for the second, and five songs left after that for the third song. Multiply.

$$7 \times 6 \times 5 = 210$$

9. Average: 19 minutes per mile

   Mode: 20 minutes per mile

   Median: 20 minutes per mile
   For the average, add them up and divide.

   $20 + 23 + 20 + 24 + 18 = 105$, and $105 \div 5 = 21$.

   For the mode, list them in order as well so the median is easier, and find the one that occurs most frequently: 18, 20, 20, 23, 24. Twenty occurs most frequently and is smack dab in the middle as well, so it is the median as well as the mode.

10. $\dfrac{1}{81}$

    Each time there is a probability of $\dfrac{1}{3}$, so to find the series of probabilities, multiply these.

    $$\frac{1}{3} \times \frac{1}{3} \times \frac{1}{3} \times \frac{1}{3} = \frac{1}{81}$$

    It isn't all that likely, is it?

✍ QUIZ #16 ✍
Reading Line Graphs

1. 50
   Look above 1987 till you see the point, then move sideways to the left axis. The number there is 50, and that is how many people learned to dive that year.

2. 1989
   The highest point of the graph gives the greatest number of people, and that is 100 people in 1989.

3. 1994
   Look to the lowest point on the graph; it's all the way to the right on 1994.

4. 1988-1989

   You are looking for the steepest rise from left to right, and it is between 1988 and 1989. You can also subtract year to year if you aren't sure.

5. 1993-1994

   Now you are looking for the steepest decline from left to right, which is between 1993 and 1994. You can again subtract and look for the greatest difference if you like.

✍ QUIZ #17 ✍
Reading Pictographs

1. 200

   Since each symbol represents 100 people, and there are two farmer symbols, this indicates that there are 200 farmers in Smalltown who like music.

2. 400

   Each symbol is 100, and there are four of them for the teachers, so 400 teachers like music.

3. There are more teachers.

   You know from questions 1 and 2 that there are 400 teachers and 200 farmers who like music, so there are more teachers in this graph, but bear in mind that this does not mean that teachers in general like music more, even in Smalltown. Why? Because it is possible that there are only 200 farms, so all the farmers like music, and it is also possible that there are 2,000 teachers, so only 10% of the teachers in Smalltown like music. With this pictograph you cannot tell.

4. There are more athletes.

   There are two athlete symbols, or 200 athletes who like music in Smalltown, and only one cowboy symbol, or only 100 cowboys in Smalltown who like music.

5. Students

   There are five student symbols, or 500 students in Smalltown who like to listen to music, more than any of the other groups represented.

✍ QUIZ #18 ✍
Reading Pie Charts

1. There are more black widows.
   How do you know? Look at the chart; the section taken up by black widows is larger, and the collection is 23% black widows, as compared to 20% daddy longlegs.

2. There are more tarantulas.
   Again, look at the graph and see which section is bigger, or which percentage—37% or 15%—is bigger. Clearly, 37% is a greater portion of the collection.

3. 23
   Well, if the whole is 100, and 23% of the whole is black widow spiders, to find the actual number of black widows just multiply: $\frac{23}{100} \times 100 = 23$.
   You would also do well to remember that when you are asked to find a certain percent of 100, since percent just means per 100, the answer is the number of the percent. In other words, 23% of 100 is 23, and 5% of 100 is 5, and so on.

4. 20
   Since daddy longlegs are 20% of the whole, and the whole is 100, there are 20 daddy longlegs in the collection.

5. 63
   There are many ways to answer this question. Some of you may have added up all the other percents and gotten 63, and that's terrific. Another quicker way is to simply subtract the tarantulas from the whole. So, the whole is 100, and there are 37 tarantulas, which leaves 63 other spiders.

✍ QUIZ #19 ✍
Chapter 7 Review

1. 700
   Look at the 1960 line, and go up to the point, and then over left to the number of people—in hundreds, remember.

2. 280
   If you got somewhere between 200 and 300, that is close enough; when you have question on a year that is not represented clearly, look at your graph and approximate.

3. 1950
   The highest point on the graph is at 1950, so that is the year in which the greatest number of people knew how to Hula Hoop.

4. 1975-1980
   The steepest rise occurs between 1975 and 1980, when there was an increase of 200 people.

5. 100
   Since each symbol represents 100 people and there is one symbol for the bowlers, 100 bowlers like coconut.

6. 400
   Four symbols represents 400 people.

7. 600
   There are seven symbols for basketball players and one symbol for bowlers, so the difference is six symbols, which represents 600 people.

8. Reading
   Reading accounts for 12% of her free time, while spacing out only accounts for 8% of her free time, therefore reading accounts for more of her free time.

9. 6 hours
   You need to find 12% of the whole, or 12% of 50.

$$\frac{12}{100} \times 50 = \frac{12}{2} \times 6$$

10. 5 hours
Combining the two activities from the start will
be easiest, they account for 10% of the whole.
Since the whole is 50, you can take 10% easily by
moving the decimal point one space to the left
and getting 5.

✍ QUIZ #20 ✍
Chapter 8 Review

1. Square
Squares have four equal sides.

2. Hexagon
Hexagons have six sides, and they are closed and
flat.

3. The diameter

4. 40°, which means it is an acute angle.
One way to make approximating easier is to
imagine a perpendicular line—that is, a line
forming a right angle—and compare the angle in
question to the right angle. First, is it greater or
smaller than the right angle? This one is smaller,
so it is acute. Then is it less than half or more
than half? This one looks to be a little less than
half, but only a little bit less, around 40°.

5. 24 cubic units
The formula to find the volume of a rectangular
solid is l × w × h. Since the length here is 2,
and the width is 4, and the height is 3,
2 × 3 × 4 gives the volume, which is 24.

6. 26
Add up the sides of the carpet, also known as
the perimeter, and you get 26.

7. 8
Look at all the following marked right angles.
Did you notice the upside-down one? An angle
has the same measurement no matter how it is
oriented in space.

8. 6 square feet
   To cover a flat piece you need to find the area that needs to be covered. Here the shape is a rectangle, so the area is the measure of the length times the width, or 2 times 3, which gives 6.

9. The best way to describe it would be to call it a cone resting on its base, with a sphere balanced on top.

10. 4p
   This question is asking you to find the circumference of the circle. The formula for circumference of a circle is p times the diameter, or pd. Since the diameter—the line from edge to edge running through the middle—is four, the circumference is 4p.

✍ QUIZ #21 ✎
Negative Numbers

1. –5 is bigger
   Take a look at a number line. Which one is closer to the positive numbers?

2. 0 is bigger
   Look at a number line again; 0 is closer to positive than –1, so it is bigger. Or think of it like this: If you have no money but don't owe anyone money either, that's better than owing someone a dollar.

3. –13 is bigger
   It can get confusing, because in the set of positive numbers, 31 would be bigger than 13, but with negative numbers everything is reversed. Or think of debt again: The more you owe, the less you have.

4. –7
   What if you dug down 3 feet and then dug another 4? You would be 7 feet deep.

5. –12

6. –3

This might have been a little tricky. Start at the positive number on the number line, then go down (like you were digging a hole down) 15 spaces for the –15. You go down past 0, to –3.

7. 1

Whew! There are many ways to look at this. You can go on the number line to –3, and then, since you are subtracting a negative number, move up 4 spaces. When subtracting a negative you can put the two minus signs to form a plus, so it's as though –3 – –4 = ? really says –3 + 4 = ?.

8. 18

Again, subtracting a negative is like adding a positive so 8 – –10 can be seen as 8 + 10.

9. –5

Start at twelve on the number line, and move down 17 spaces. You end up at –5. Or for a quick fix, just reverse the numbers and add a negative sign to the difference, 12 – 17 becomes 17 – 12 = 5, so the answer is –5.

10. 5

Subtracting a negative is like adding a positive, so 3 – –2 becomes 3 + 2, which is equal to 5.

✍ QUIZ #22 ✍
Multiplying and Dividing Negative Numbers

1. –12

A negative times a positive is a negative.

2. 22

A negative times a negative is a positive. Don't these rules get irritating?

3. 64

4. 0

Anything, whether positive or negative, times 0 is equal to 0.

5. –20

6. 22

A negative divided by a negative yields a positive answer.

7. –5

A positive number divided by a negative number will give a negative number as the answer.

8. –4

Same reason as the question above this one.

9. 0

Zero divided by any number, negative or positive, is equal to 0. If you have nothing to divide up, how many piles will you divide it into? None!

10. 2

A negative number divided by a negative number? Why, positive, of course.

✍ QUIZ #23 ✍
Chapter 9 Review

1. –1

What a pain! Just go at it one step at a time and remember PEMDAS. First, parentheses.

$$3 + -4(2 - 1) =$$

becomes

$$3 + -4(1)=$$

Then, since there are no exponents, any multiplication or division gets done left to right.

$$3 + -4(1)=$$

becomes

$$3 + -4 =$$

And $3 + -4 = -1$. Use your number line if you like.

2. –14

Since there is only addition and subtraction here, you do this problem left to right. Starting at –5, then less 7, so go down 7 to –12, and then less another 2, down to –14.

3. −4

This problem contains only multiplication and division, which you know from PEMDAS is done left to right. So, −6 divided by −3 is 2, then 2 times −2 is equal to −4.

4. 0

Left to right, you're just bouncing back and forth on the number line. Any number plus itself in the negative form is equal to 0, right? 5 + −5, or −6 + 6. How else could you write this problem? How about 2(−1 + 1)? Because you do the same operation two times! Cool, isn't it?

5. −3

Bring out your old pal PEMDAS and get to work. What is first? Why, parentheses, of course.

$$-2(-3 + -4) - 17 =$$

becomes

$$-2(-7) - 17 =$$

Next is multiplication, which leaves you with this:

$$14 - 17 =$$

You can now just reverse them and add on a negative sign, or move it onto the number line to see what happens. Think about it, the 14 and the −14 inside the −17 cancel each other out, and all you are left with is the extra −3 from the −17.

6. 12

Division first, which gives you 5, then 5 plus 7 is 12.

7. −80

Multiplication and division go straight left to right, so −32 times 5 is −160, divided by 2 is −80.

8. 35

Another pain in the neck, but simple once you break it down into steps. First, the parentheses:

$$17 + 23 - -5(2 - 3) =$$

becomes

$$17 + 23 - -5(-1) =$$

Then any multiplication or division.

$$17 + 23 - -5(-1) =$$

becomes

$$17 + 23 - 5 =$$

That works because –5 times –1 becomes a positive, in fact, 5. Now, the addition and subtraction is straight left to right.

9. –1

Switch those babies around and add a negative sign.

10. 71

Subtracting a negative is like adding a positive. You are getting rid of debt, or filling up a dug hole, or however you want to view it. So put those two signs together and form a plus sign, and add the numbers.

✍ QUIZ #24 ✍
Algebra

1. 4

2. 2

3. 6

4. 6

This is exactly the same expression as question 3. The parentheses aren't written (because mathematicians can be lazy too), but you should know when you see $2x$, it can be thought of as $2(x)$.

5. –3

$-x$ is exactly the same as $-1x$ is exactly the same as –1 times x. They all mean the same thing.

6. 4

Remember, $-2 - 2 = -4$. How much is –2 *times* –2? Positive 4

7. 6

A negative times a negative is a positive! Always.

8. 4

Plug in –2 for the variables and you should get this: –8 – (–12), that's the same as –8 + 12. Which of course gives 4 as the answer.

9. 7

10. 9

Remember PEMDAS! Parentheses first: $x + 3 = 15$. That negative sign outside the parentheses turns (15) into –15. Multiplication comes next: $2 \times 12 = 24$. Now the problem is simply $24 - 15$.

✍ QUIZ #25 ✍
Review

1. $x = 4$

All you needed to do was *subtract* 3 from *both* sides.

2. $x = 10$

Because you add 9 to both sides.

3. $x = 4$

Divide both sides by 3.

4. $x = 4$

Divide both sides by –3. –3 divided by –3 is 1, because a negative divided by a negative is positive, and the 3's cancel out. –12 divided by –3 is the same as 12 divided by 3. 4. Again, because both numbers are negative, and we're doing multiplication or division, the answer is positive.

5. $x = 1$

Combine the two x's. $x + x$ is $2x$. $2x + 2 = 4$. Subtract 2 from both sides. (Remember adding or subtracting is the next step.) Then divide both sides by 2. There you have $\frac{2}{2} = x$. $\frac{2}{2}$ is the same as 1, because any number divided by itself equals 1.

6. $x = 3$

   Combine $+3x$ with $-x$. That's $2x$. Now subtract seven from both sides. That leaves $2x = 6$. Divide both sides by 2. X does indeed equal three.

7. $x = 12$

   Remember to multiply both sides by the denominator first. (Because there's nothing to combine, or you'd combine first.) That leaves $3x = 36$. Now it's simple: Divide both sides by 3.

8. $x = 2$

   Again, there's nothing to combine. This one's tricky. Multiply both sides by x—that leaves $20 = 10x$. See how that works. On the left side the x's cancel, on the right side x times 10 is $10x$. Now divide both sides by 10.

9. $x = \dfrac{1}{4}$

   Start by subtracting 4 from each side. That leaves $\dfrac{7}{2x} = 14$. Multiply both sides by $2x$. That leaves $7 = 28x$. Divide both sides by 28. That leaves $\dfrac{7}{28} = x$, and $\dfrac{7}{28}$ reduces to $\dfrac{1}{4}$.

10. $x = 3$

    Combine first. The fractions can be added because they have the same denominator. So, combined the value is $\dfrac{11x}{3}$. Now multiply both sides by 3. That leaves $\dfrac{11x}{33}$. Divide both sides by 11. There you go.

    Great job!

✍ NOTES ✍

NOTES

✍ NOTES ✍

ABOUT THE AUTHORS

Marcia Lerner graduated from Brown University in 1986. She is the author of *Writing Smart* and *Math Smart*, and has been teaching and writing for The Princeton Review since 1988. She lives in Brooklyn, N.Y.

Doug McMullen, Jr. is a writer who has, among other things, worked for the circus and harvested wildflowers. He has taught for The Princeton Review since 1988.